232
225
4.57

238   1
237
4.75   1.
4.57
4.
8.32

HBJ Reading Program

Margaret Early

Bernice E. Cullinan
Roger C. Farr
W. Dorsey Hammond
Nancy Santeusanio
Dorothy S. Strickland

LEVEL 6

Streamers

HBJ **HARCOURT BRACE JOVANOVICH, PUBLISHERS**
Orlando   San Diego   Chicago   Dallas

Acknowledgments

For permission to reprint copyrighted material, grateful acknowledgment is made to the following sources:

Atheneum Publishers, Inc.: "Bedtime" from *8 a.m. Shadows* by Patricia Hubbell. Copyright © 1965 by Patricia Hubbell.
Curtis Brown, Ltd.: Adapted from *The Simple Prince* by Jane Yolen. Copyright © 1978 by Jane Yolen. Published by Parents' Magazine Press.
Carolrhoda Books, Inc., 241 First Avenue North, Minneapolis, MN 55401: From *Cornstalks and Cannonballs* by Barbara Mitchell. Copyright © 1980 by Carolrhoda Books, Inc.
Coward, McCann & Geoghegan: Adapted from *Forecast* by Malcolm Hall. Text copyright © 1977 by Malcolm Hall.
E. P. Dutton, a division of New American Library: Adapted from *Clyde Monster* by Robert L. Crowe, illustrated by Kay Chorao. Text copyright © 1976 by Robert L. Crowe; illustrations copyright © 1976 by Kap Sproat Chorao.
E. P. Dutton, a division of New American Library and The Canadian Publishers, McClelland and Stewart Limited, Toronto: "Politeness" from *When We Were Very Young* by A. A. Milne. Copyright 1924 by E. P. Dutton; renewed 1952 by A. A. Milne.
Greenwillow Books, a division of William Morrow & Company, Inc.: Abridged and adapted from *Jenny and the Tennis Nut* by Janet Schulman. Copyright © 1978 by Janet Schulman.
Harcourt Brace Jovanovich, Inc.: Abridged and adapted from the text of *Jane Martin Dog Detective* by Eve Bunting. Copyright © 1984 by Eve Bunting. Abridged and adapted from the text of *Sun Up, Sun Down* by Gail Gibbons. Copyright © 1983 by Gail Gibbons.
Harper & Row, Publishers, Inc.: Complete text, abridged and adapted, and illustrations from *Arthur's Honey Bear* by Lillian Hoban. Copyright © 1974 by Lillian Hoban. Complete text, abridged and adapted, and illustrations from *Barkley,* written and illustrated by Syd Hoff. Copyright © 1975 by Syd Hoff. Text and illustrations from "Owl and the Moon" in *Owl at Home,* written and illustrated by Arnold Lobel. Copyright © 1975 by Arnold Lobel.
Holt, Rinehart and Winston, Publishers: "Keepsakes" from *Is Somewhere Always Far Away?* by Leland B. Jacobs. Copyright © 1967 by Leland B. Jacobs.
Jane W. Krows: "The New Year" by Jane W. Krows.
G. P. Putnam's Sons: Adapted from *The Quilt Story* by Tony Johnston, pictures by Tomie dePaola. Text © 1985 by Tony Johnston; illustrations © 1985 by Tomie dePaola.
Marian Reiner, as agent for Myra Cohn Livingston: "My Dog" from *The Moon and a Star and Other Poems* by Myra Cohn Livingston. Copyright © 1965 by Myra Cohn Livingston.
Charles Scribner's Sons: Adapted from *How the Sun Made a Promise and Kept It* by Margery Bernstein and Janet Kobrin. Copyright © 1972, 1974 by Margery Bernstein and Janet Kobrin.
Karen S. Solomon: "Change in the Weather" by Ilo Orleans.
Viking Penguin Inc.: Adapted from *Watch Out, Ronald Morgan!* by Patricia Reilly Giff. Copyright © 1985 by Patricia Reilly Giff.
Franklin Watts, Inc.: From *Beatrice Doesn't Want To* by Laura Joffe Numeroff. Text copyright © 1981 by Laura Joffe Numeroff. Adapted from *Let's Find Out About New Year's Day* (Titled: "New Year's Day") by Martha and Charles Shapp. Text copyright © 1968 by Franklin Watts, Inc.
Albert Whitman & Company: From *Nick Joins In,* written and illustrated by Joe Lasker. Copyright © 1980 by Joe Lasker. From *Grandma Without Me,* written and illustrated by Judith Vigna. Text and illustrations © 1984 by Judith Vigna. Both published by Albert Whitman & Company.

Key: (l) – Left; (r) – Right; (c) – Center; (t) – Top; (b) – Bottom

Photographs

Cover: HBJ Photo/John Petrey

Page 2, Ed Cooper; 3 (l), Culver Pictures; 3 (r) J.M. Mejuto/FPG; 56 (l), HBJ Photo/Richard Stacks, Courtesy of the San Francisco S.P.C.A. Hearing Dog Program; 56 (r), HBJ Photo/Richard Stacks, Courtesy of Guide Dogs For The Blind, San Rafael; 57 (all), HBJ Photo/Richard Stacks; 58 (both), HBJ Photo/Richard Stacks; 59, HBJ Photo/Richard Stacks; 60, HBJ Photo/Richard Stacks; 63, Ed Cooper; 66, Colour Library International; 67, P. Kresan/H. Armstrong Roberts; 127, P. Kresan/H. Armstrong Roberts; 130 (tl), Joel Gordon; 130 (lc), Comstock; 130 (bl), Joel Gordon; 130 (c), Joel Gordon; 130 (tr), Joel Gordon; 130 (rc), Joel Gordon; 130 (br), Joel Gordon; 131, HBJ Photo; 168, H. Armstrong Roberts; 169, Phil Degginger/Bruce Coleman, Inc.; 170 (l), Roger Minkoff/Animals, Animals; 170 (r), Scott Camazine/Photo Researchers; 171, E.R. Degginger; 172, H. Armstrong Roberts; 184 (l), M. Fogden/Bruce Coleman, Inc.; 184 (r), J.H. Robinson/Photo Researchers; 185 (tl), M. Williams/Photo Nats; 185 (bl), D. Overcash/Bruce Coleman, Inc.; 185 (tr), L. Stone/Bruce Coleman, Inc.; 185 (br), J. & D. Bartlett/Bruce Coleman, Inc.; 186 (l), E.R. Degginger; 186 (r), National Audubon Society/Photo Researchers; 187, M. Williams/Photo Nats; 188, E.R. Degginger; 195, HBJ Photo; 198-199, HBJ Photo/John Petrey; 212, HBJ Photo/Rodney Jones; 213, HBJ Photo/Rodney Jones; 214, HBJ Photo/Rodney Jones; 215, HBJ Photo/Rodney Jones; 216, HBJ Photo/Rodney Jones; 273, HBJ Photo/John Petrey

continued on page 294

Printed in the United States of America

ISBN 0-15-330506-1

Contents

Unit 3 # Kaleidoscopes **130**

Streamers

Unit 1

Stepping Stones

In "Stepping Stones," you will read about many things. All of the people in these stories are doing something new. They may be trying something for the very first time. They may also be looking at old things in another way.

As you read "Stepping Stones," think about how the people in each story take a step to make friends or to learn about others. See how they learn from these new happenings. See what fun it can be to try something new!

3

Ronald Morgan needs glasses. He thinks that the glasses will make him a superkid. What does Ronald find out?

Watch Out, Ronald Morgan!

by Patricia Reilly Giff

It all started when I raced across the school yard and slid on a patch of ice.

"Watch out!" Rosemary yelled. But it was too late. I bumped into her, and she landed in a snow pile.

After I hung up my coat, I fed the goldfish. I fed Frank, the gerbil, too.

"Oh, no," Rosemary said. "You fed the gerbil food to Goldie!"

"The boxes look the same," I said.

Billy shook his head. "Can't you read the letters? *F* is for fish. *G* is for gerbil."

"It's all right," said my friend Michael. He put more water into the fish tank.

After lunch we looked outside. Everything was white. "It's time for a winter classroom," said Miss Tyler. I sat down and drew a snowflake. Then I cut it out.

Tom said, "Ronald Morgan, that's a funny snowflake. Why don't you cut on the lines?"

When it was time to go, Miss Tyler gave me a note to take home. "Maybe you need glasses," she said.

At lunch the next day, Marc asked, "When do you get your glasses?"

"I go to Doctor Sims's office today," I answered.

Michael asked, "Can I go with you?"

When we got to Doctor Sims's office, Doctor Sims said, "Look at these E's. Which way do they point?" I pointed. Then the E's looked smaller and smaller. Doctor Sims said, "It's hard for you to see them."

My mother said, "You'll look great in glasses."

"Yes," said Doctor Sims. "Glasses will help. They'll make everything look sharp and clear."

I tried on red frames. They slid down over my nose. Then I put on blue frames.

"Good," said my mother.

"Good," said Michael.

Then Doctor Sims said, "The glasses will be ready in a little while."

When my glasses were ready, I said, "I'll be the superkid of the school."

Before school, I threw some snowballs.
"You missed!" Jimmy yelled.

Michael said, "How come your glasses
don't work?"

In the classroom, I hung up my coat
and put my hat away.

"Where is our fish person?" asked Miss
Tyler.

I ran to give Goldie some food. This
time I looked at the box. The letters
looked big and sharp. "*G* is for Goldie," I
said. "*F* is for Frank."

"Oh, no," said Billy. "*F* is for fish. *G* is
for gerbil."

Michael said, "I don't think your
glasses help."

8

I put the glasses inside my hat.

Alice looked at me. "Why aren't you wearing your blue glasses?" she asked.

I shook my head. "My glasses don't work. I'll never be the superkid of the class."

When it was time to go home, Miss Tyler gave me another note. My mother helped me with some of the words.

I know you are sad about your glasses. Glasses will not make you throw better. You have to keep throwing a ball again and again. Also, you'll still trip if you don't watch out. Glasses help you see better. They make everything sharp and clear. Please wear your glasses.   Love, Miss Tyler
P.S. You ARE a super kid.

In school the next day, I drew a snowman and cut it out. "Hey," I said, "Miss Tyler's right. The lines are sharp and clear."

"Good snowman," said Rosemary.

Miss Tyler said, "Just what we need for our winter classroom."

I drew blue glasses on my snowman. "Now he's a super snowman," I said. We all clapped.

1. What does Ronald find out about his glasses?

2. Why did Ronald draw glasses on his snowman?

3. How did Miss Tyler help Ronald get used to his new glasses?

4. When did you first begin to think that Ronald's glasses weren't going to solve his problems?

Think about the things that went wrong for Ronald before he got his glasses. Write sentences that tell about three of those things.

Benjamin Franklin discovered many things that are still used by many people today. How did Benjamin Franklin help some people see better?

Benjamin Franklin's Glasses

by Sally McMillan

Benjamin Franklin did many things. He was a printer. He discovered electricity. He also liked to write books and newspapers. He even helped to write some of the first laws for the United States.

Benjamin stopped going to school when he was only ten years old. He had to go to work. Benjamin still wanted to learn, even if he was not in school. He learned many things just by reading. He was always reading. He read anything he could find.

Benjamin Franklin was always coming up with new ideas. One of his ideas was the Franklin stove. He made a stove that stood inside a fireplace. It made a room much hotter than a fireplace did. Even today, people use stoves that are very much like the stove that Franklin made.

As Franklin grew older, he found he needed glasses. He needed one pair of glasses to see things that were near. He needed another pair of glasses to see things that were far away.

"I want to read books. I want to look at fire, water, and the stars. I don't want two pairs of glasses. I want just one pair so that I can see both near and far away," he said.

So Franklin took the top part of his glasses for faraway things. He took the bottom part of his glasses for near things. Then Franklin put them together and made one new pair of glasses.

Franklin put on the glasses.

"This is what I need," he said.

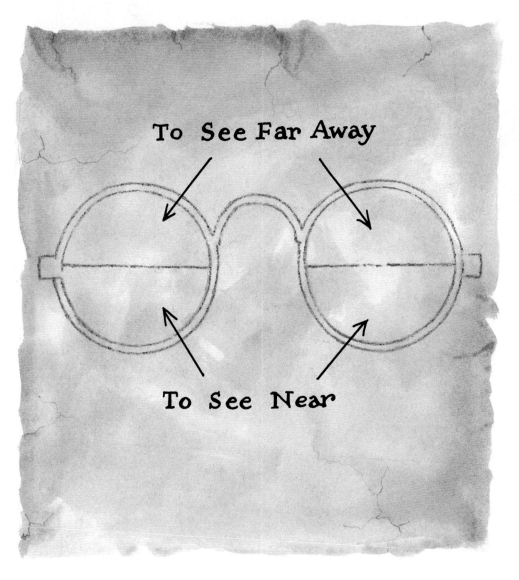

To See Far Away

To See Near

"When I look up, I can see things that are far away. When I look down, I can see things that are near. I think I will call my new glasses bifocals." With his new glasses Franklin kept on reading and learning.

Benjamin Franklin made bifocals so that people needed only one pair of glasses to see both near and far away. The bifocals that people wear today are very much like the ones Franklin made many years ago.

1. How did Benjamin Franklin help some people see better?

2. What kind of glasses did Benjamin Franklin make?

3. Why did Benjamin need a new kind of glasses?

4. What part of the story made you think that Benjamin Franklin would make bifocal glasses?

Think and Write

Benjamin Franklin left school when he was ten. Write sentences to tell how he learned so much without going to school. Tell about some of his ideas.

17

Nick is going to school with other children for the first time. What does Nick think of the school and the new friends he meets there?

Nick Joins In

story and pictures by Joe Lasker

Nick was afraid. Soon he would be going to school. No longer would a teacher come to his home.

Nick talked to his parents. "How can I go to school in my wheelchair?" he asked. "What if the kids don't like me? Will there be anyone else in the school who can't walk?"

On and on, Nick's questions spilled out. "We know why you feel so afraid," his parents said. Nick felt a little better.

On Wednesday morning a small yellow bus took Nick to his school. A teacher met the bus. "We hope you like our school, Nick," she said. The teacher pushed Nick down a long hall and into his new classroom.

Everyone in the room looked at Nick. His teacher, Mrs. Becker, smiled at him. "We're glad you're here," she said. Then she told Nick the names of the boys and girls in the class.

No one spoke. Then Mrs. Becker said, "Nick, I think the children would like to ask you some questions. Is that all right?" Nick nodded, looking down.

Rachel asked the first question.

"Why do you have to use a wheelchair?"

"Because I can't walk," Nick said.

"Why can't you walk?" asked Nina.

"Because my legs didn't grow right."

"Why is that?" asked Timmie.

Nick looked at him. "I've always been this way."

Then Mrs. Becker said, "All right, boys and girls, it's time to get back to work." Then she helped Nick get started.

Nick looked at all the children, at his teacher, and at the bright pictures on the walls. He didn't feel so afraid anymore. He felt he might like this school.

Days went by. Nick and the other children grew used to each other. They learned from one another.

Without being asked, people helped Nick. He helped people, too. Sometimes Nick helped the gym teacher open windows with the long window pole.

Nick made friends. One of them was
Timmie. Nick loved to go outside with
the other children.

For the first time in his life, Nick
played outdoor games. He couldn't run
like Timmie, but he moved fast.

What Nick wished for most was to play
ball like the others. How fast and high
they ran and jumped! To Nick, that was
like flying.

One afternoon there was a ball game in the school yard. The ball went higher and higher. It landed on the roof of the gym. The ball rolled to the edge of the roof and got stuck. All the children groaned.

Timmie threw a big ball to try to move the ball that was stuck. But the ball didn't move. A teacher put Ben onto his shoulders, but Ben couldn't get the ball down.

Nick had an idea. So he left the
playground. He went into the open gym,
past the tall gym windows, and went
right to where the window pole was. He
took the pole and went back outside.

The children were still looking at the stuck ball. Then Nina saw Nick coming. "Nick to the rescue!" she shouted. "In the nick of time!"

"Excuse me, please," said Nick. He held the window pole. No one was going to take it from him! He stopped under the edge of the roof. He held the pole up and poked the ball. The ball dropped down.

"Nick to the rescue!" everyone shouted.

Nick felt as if he were flying.

1. How did Nick feel about his new school? Why?

2. What did Nick do that the children could not do?

3. What did the children find out about helping one another?

4. Read the sentence that tells how Nick felt when he got the ball down.

Think about why going to a new school scared Nick. How could you help him? Write a paragraph that tells three things you could do to help Nick.

Someone

by Carol Quinn

Someone came
To school today,
Someone new
From far away.
Someone quiet,
Someone shy,
Who watches as
We hurry by.

Someone lonely,
Someone who
Is frightened by
A place that's new.
I'll invite
That someone new
To join in
Everything I do.
And when the busy
School day ends,
Someone new
Will share my friends.

29

Draw Conclusions

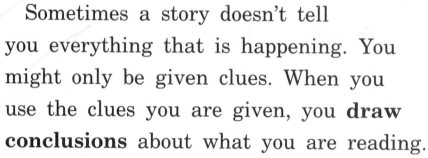

Sometimes a story doesn't tell you everything that is happening. You might only be given clues. When you use the clues you are given, you **draw conclusions** about what you are reading.

Read the following paragraph. Look for clues to help you draw conclusions about what Nina's friends were doing.

All of Nina's friends were at her house. There were hats, balloons, and gifts. When Nina came home, they all shouted, "Surprise!"

What were Nina's friends doing? They were giving her a party. How did you know this? The hats, balloons, and gifts are all clues.

Now read this paragraph. Look for the clues that tell you where Peter is.

Peter walked and walked. He stopped and looked at all the different animals. Peter saw some seals. He saw some elephants, too. Peter liked the elephants best of all.

Where was Peter? How did you know this? The clues in the paragraph are *walked and walked, saw some seals,* and *saw some elephants*. These clues should have helped you know that Peter was at the zoo.

Looking for clues in a story or a paragraph can help you understand what you read. Now you are going to read a selection about a missing dog. Look for clues to help you find the missing dog.

Jane Martin likes to help people solve problems. What clues does Jane use as she tries to solve the case of the missing dog?

Jane Martin, Dog Detective

by Eve Bunting

Jane pinned the sign on the pole. It said:

Have you lost a dog?
Let me find it for you.
Jane Martin, Dog Detective
23 Oak Street
(My treehouse is at the back.)

Fee 25 cents a day

Jane had made ten signs. This was
the last one. Now she could go home
and wait. Jane did not have to wait
long. A boy yelled from under a tree,
"Are you the dog detective?"

"Yes," said Jane as she came down
from her tree house. She had on her
dog detective badge.

"I am Tim Wilson," the boy said.
"My dog, Charlie, is missing."

Jane wrote in her notebook: Case
one—find Charlie, the missing dog.
"I will need to know everything about
Charlie," Jane said.

"Charlie was not in his doghouse this morning," Tim told her. "Someone left this note."

Jane read the note:

> *I took Charlie. I will take good care of him.*

"We will go to your house. I will look for clues," said Jane.

Tim showed her Charlie's doghouse.

"The person who took Charlie also took his dish, his bone, and his hoop," said Tim.

Jane said, "There might be a clue here. What does Charlie do with his hoop?"

"He can push his hoop with his nose. Charlie is smart. He can even count. When I ask how old he is, he barks four times. Charlie always wins the Smartest Dog prize at the dog show. The show is next week. I hope you can find him by then."

Tim showed Jane a picture of Charlie. He was small and white.

"I am thinking," Jane said. "Someone wants to put Charlie in the show, and Charlie will get the first prize. We must see the list of the dogs that will be in the dog show."

The dog-show man told them the
names and kinds of dogs in the show.

"I need to see Rover, Biff, and
Flash," Jane said.

"You don't have to see Flash," Tim
said. "Flash is Susie's dog. He is not
a very smart dog. He barks when there
is no one at the door. When someone
is there, Flash never barks. Why did
Susie put him in the dog show?"

Jane said, "I will find Charlie. You
go home now, Tim."

She went to Rover's house. Rover
had long, long ears. "You can't be
Charlie," Jane said.

She went to Biff's house. Biff was
very, very small. "You can't be Charlie,"
Jane said.

"Flash is the only dog left on the
list," she thought, "and Tim knows
Flash. So Susie could not change
Charlie for Flash. But why would Susie
put Flash . . ." Jane stopped. "Oh!" she
cried. She felt like a real detective.

Jane ran to Flash's house. She rang the bell. A dog barked. Susie came to the door.

"Hi," Jane said. She showed Susie her dog detective badge. "I want to see Flash."

"Why?" Susie asked.

"I am on a big case," Jane said.

"Flash! Flash!" Susie called. No dog came. "I will have to get him," Susie said. She came back with a little dog. He could have been Charlie, but he wasn't white.

Susie put the dog down. "Sit," she said. The dog didn't sit. "Up," Susie said. The dog sat down.

"I can see that this is not Charlie," Jane said. "This dog is not very smart. He must be Flash."

Jane knew that Susie had Charlie. She thought about what Tim had told her.

"How old are you, Charlie?" she cried. From the back of the house came four barks. Charlie had answered.

"The game is over," Jane told Susie. "Bring Charlie to me."

Susie was afraid. "How did you know?" she asked Jane.

"When I rang the doorbell, a dog barked. Flash does not bark when someone comes to the door."

Just then a small white dog ran into the room. "Bark once if you are Charlie," Jane said. The little dog barked once.

"How did you get out?" Susie asked.

"He's a smart dog," Jane said.

Someone rang the doorbell. It was Tim. He ran in when Susie opened the door. Charlie ran right to Tim.

"Oh, Charlie! Charlie!" Tim said.
"I could not stay home," he told Jane.
"I followed you. Then I heard Charlie
bark. Why did you take him, Susie?"

"I was going to give Charlie back,
but first I wanted him to teach Flash
some tricks. I want Flash to be a smart
dog, too."

"That is why she took the hoop,"
Jane told Tim. "Charlie could use the
hoop to teach Flash."

"If you had asked me, I would have helped you," Tim said to Susie. "All dogs can learn. I can teach Flash. Do you want me to?"

"Yes, please," Susie said.

"Then I won't say anything to anyone," Tim said. "But you can pay Jane for finding Charlie."

Jane opened her notebook. She wrote:

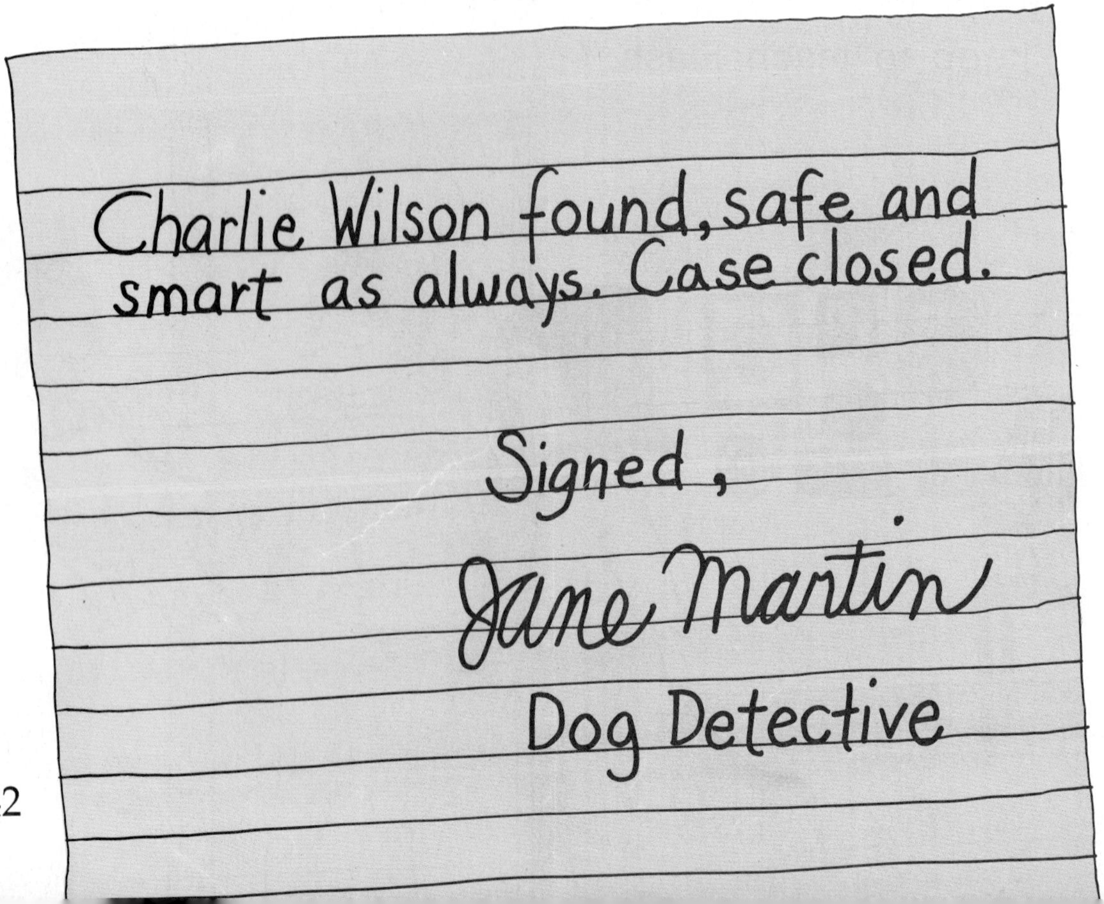

Charlie Wilson found, safe and smart as always. Case closed.

Signed,

Jane Martin

Dog Detective

1. What clues did Jane use in the case of the missing dog?

2. Why did Jane ask questions about Charlie and the other dogs?

3. Why did Jane want to see the list of dogs in the show?

4. Where in the story did you think Charlie was at Susie's house?

Think

and

Write

Jane helped Tim because Tim told her all about his dog. Think about another animal. Write three sentences that tell about the animal so someone else could find it if it were lost.

Reality and Fantasy

Stories that people make up are called **fiction.** If a story could be real or true, it is called **realistic.** Made-up stories that we think could happen are called **realistic fiction.** The story "Nick Joins In" is made up, but Nick seems like a real boy. The things he says and does are just like the things you might say and do.

Some stories we read could not really happen. We call these stories **fantasy.** Fantasy stories may be about people who do things that could not really happen. They may also be about animals that can do things that people do. In fantasy stories, animals may talk, drive cars, cook, and dance.

Read the following sentences. Which would be in a realistic story? Which would be in a fantasy? Why?

1. Three bears went to a party.
2. Ben rode a yellow bike to school.

Sentence 1 is fantasy because bears can't go to a party. Sentence 2 is realistic because someone really could ride a yellow bike to school.

Now read these sentences. Decide which would be in a realistic story. Decide which would be in a fantasy. Tell why.

3. Mr. Fig used his magic hat to fly up into the sky.
4. Jane went right home after school.

As you read the next selection, try to decide if it is a realistic story or a fantasy and why.

Barkley thought he was too old to stay with the circus. Where does Barkley go? What happens to him?

Barkley

story and pictures by Syd Hoff

Barkley had a job in the circus. He did tricks with four other dogs. Barkley walked on his front legs. He walked on his back legs. The other dogs stood on Barkley's back and jumped off. If one of the dogs did something wrong, Barkley barked!

46

Barkley always led the way when the
dogs walked on a rope. Everyone
clapped and yelled, and Barkley took a
bow. Then he played with the children.
Barkley liked that best of all.

One day, when the four dogs jumped on Barkley's back, it hurt! Another day, Barkley walked too slowly. The other dogs went in front of him. "I will be all right," thought Barkley, but he could not take a bow.

"I think you are getting old," said Barkley's owner. "That happens to all of us." The next day, Barkley's owner said, "I don't want you to get hurt. Another dog is taking your place."

Barkley saw the other dog doing his tricks. The other dog did them very well.

Barkley missed the clapping, and he missed the yelling. He missed the children most of all. "There must be something I can do," he thought.

Barkley tried to work with the seals, but the ball would not stay on his nose. He tried to do tricks with the elephants, but he just got in their way.

"There is nothing I can do here," he thought. So when no one was looking, Barkley left the circus.

Barkley walked and walked for a long time. He wanted some food. "If I do a trick," he thought, "maybe someone will give me a bone."

He walked on his front legs. He walked on his back legs. No one gave him a bone. He saw a bone in a trash can, but someone came and took the bone away.

Barkley saw some children playing.
He was so happy that he did some tricks
for them. The children played with him,
and they gave him food and water.

The children liked Barkley so much
that they wanted to keep him. "We
cannot keep you," said a girl. "There is
only one place for a smart dog like you."
She took Barkley back to the circus!

"Where were you?" asked his owner. "I missed you. I didn't want you to leave the circus. We need you to teach young dogs your tricks."

Barkley was very happy! He started his new job the next day. Barkley showed his tricks to the young dogs. When a young dog did something wrong, Barkley barked.

Now Barkley had more time to play with the children. He never wanted to leave the circus again.

1. What did Barkley do after he left the circus?

2. Do you think the girl should have taken Barkley back to the circus? Why?

3. What words in the story show that the circus owner likes Barkley?

Barkley was too old to do tricks, but he was still needed to teach the young dogs. What can a child learn from an older person? Write a paragraph that tells three things an older person can teach a young child.

My Dog

by Myra Cohn Livingston

He didn't bark *at* anything —
   a cat,
   a bird,
   a piece of string,
   a siren or a silly toad,
   a pick-up truck along the road,
   a fence,
   a bone,
   a chewed-up shoe —
He barked because he *wanted* to.

Did you know that dogs can help people? Find out how dogs do this.

Dogs at Work

by Phyllis Hoffman

Did you know that some dogs have jobs? They do not work at a circus or do tricks at home. Their jobs are to help people.

Some dogs help blind people. Other dogs help deaf people.

The dogs that help the blind are called Seeing Eye dogs. These dogs must go to special schools where they learn many things. The person who wants the Seeing Eye dog must also go to the same school.

The school only picks special kinds of dogs. The dogs must be smart and about one year old. They must like people and listen well. They must sit, come, and stay when told.

Each Seeing Eye dog is fitted with a special bar. The dog learns to walk in front of the teacher and to cross streets. The dog must also learn not to play with other dogs when it is working.

When the blind person comes to the school, he or she must learn how to take care of the dog. The blind person must also learn to tell the dog what to do. The person and the dog work hard together. When they have learned to work with each other, the dog and its owner are ready to go home.

Dogs that are trained as hearing ear dogs listen very well and must be very smart.

At school, these dogs learn to follow hand signals. These hand signals are the "words" that the deaf people will use to tell a dog what to do. The dogs must learn to listen for special sounds. When the doorbell rings, the dog must learn to pull the deaf person to the door. In the morning when the clock goes off, the hearing ear dog knows to wake up its owner.

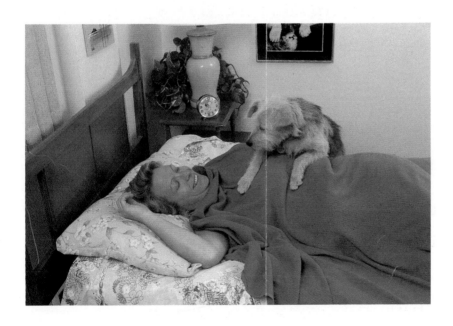

Many hearing ear dogs must also learn how to tell parents if a baby is crying. A hearing ear dog learns to listen for many sounds.

Seeing Eye and hearing ear dogs are very special. They work hard to help people. They are also loving pets!

1. What are two ways that dogs help people?

2. Tell two things a Seeing Eye dog must do.

3. Tell two things a hearing ear dog must do.

4. On what page did you learn about hand signals?

You have read about dogs at work. What other animals have jobs? Choose one animal and write three sentences about it. Where does the animal work? What job does the animal do?

61

Thinking About "Stepping Stones"

In "Stepping Stones," you read about many people who tried doing new things. It took Ronald some time to get used to having glasses. Nick was afraid before he went to school, but liked it in a short time. Barkley was sad about getting older, but he found a new job that made him happy.

Taking a step in a new direction may be a problem, but it may turn out to be lots of fun. As you read other stories, think about the people in the stories and what they learn by taking a step in a new direction.

1. What new thing did Ronald Morgan need that Benjamin Franklin needed, too?

2. How are Nick and Ronald Morgan alike? How are they different?

3. Would Barkley have been a good dog to train for one of the jobs in "Dogs at Work"? Why?

4. Why might the circus owner have called Jane Martin about Barkley?

Read on Your Own

Arthur's Eyes by Marc Brown. Little, Brown. Arthur gets glasses and his friends make fun of them. He is hurt but learns that he really needs his glasses.

Clancy's Coat by Eve Bunting. Warne. Two friends have a fight and don't talk to one another for a long time. An old coat brings them back together.

The Skate Patrol by Eve Bunting. Whitman. The Skate Patrol helps track down the Creep Thief. This story is fun to read.

Benjamin Franklin by Ingri D'Aulaire and Edgar P. Parin. Doubleday. This book is about Benjamin Franklin. It has many pretty pictures that help tell the story of Franklin's life.

Dogs Working for People by Joanna Foster.
National Geographic. This book tells
about a lot of work that dogs can do.
There are sheep dogs, rescue dogs, and
many other kinds of dogs.

Danny and the Dinosaur by Syd Hoff.
Harper. This is a funny story about a
boy who makes friends with a dinosaur.
They go for a walk around town.

Sammy the Seal by Syd Hoff. Harper.
Sammy is the only seal in the zoo who
is not happy. One day he leaves to see
what the world is like.

He's My Brother by Joe Lasker. Whitman. A
boy talks about his younger brother,
Jamie, who finds it hard to learn.

Unit 2

Earth and Sky

In "Earth and Sky," you will read about both the earth and the sky. You will learn many different things about our world.

How does the sun give us food and light here on Earth? What special trip does a raindrop take? What might happen if the sun came too near the earth?

As you read "Earth and Sky," think about some ways that the earth and the sky work together. Think about how some of the people in the stories feel about the earth and the sky.

Clyde doesn't like the nighttime because he is afraid of the dark. Why is Clyde afraid? How do his parents help him solve his problem?

Clyde Monster

by Robert L. Crowe

Clyde wasn't a very, very old monster, but he was growing uglier every day. He lived in a large forest with his parents.

Father Monster was a big, big monster
and very ugly, which was good. Friends
and family sometimes make fun of a pretty
monster. Mother Monster was even
uglier. All in all, they were a picture
family—as monsters go.

Clyde lived in a cave. That is, at
night he was supposed to live in a cave.
In the daytime, he played in the forest.
He did monster things like breathing fire
at the lake.

He also did Clyde things like jumping up and down. This made large holes in the ground. He was always bumping into things, too.

When Clyde was supposed to go to his cave and sleep, the problem started. He didn't want to go to his cave.

"Why?" asked his mother. "Why won't you go to your cave?"

"Because," answered Clyde, "I'm afraid of the dark."

"Afraid?" asked his father. "A monster of mine afraid? What are you afraid of?"

"People," said Clyde. "I'm afraid there are people in there who will get me."

"That's silly," said his father. "Come, I'll show you." His father breathed out so much fire that it lit up the cave. "There. Did you see any people?"

"No, but they may be hiding under a rock. They'll jump out and get me after I'm sleeping," answered Clyde.

"That is silly," said his mother. "There are no people here. Even if there were, they wouldn't hurt you."

"They wouldn't?" asked Clyde.

"No," said his mother. "Would you ever hide in the dark under a bed to scare a boy or girl?"

"No!" answered Clyde, upset that his mother would even think that.

"Well, people wouldn't hide and scare you. A long time ago monsters and people made a deal," said his father. "Monsters won't scare people—and people won't scare monsters."

"Really?" Clyde asked.

"Yes," said his mother. "Do you know of a monster who was ever scared by a person?"

"No," answered Clyde after some thought.

"Do you know of any boys or girls who were ever scared by a monster?"

"No," he answered.

"There!" said his mother. "Now off to bed."

"No more talk about being scared by people," said his father.

"All right, but could you keep the rock open just a little?" Clyde asked as he went into his cave.

1. Why was Clyde afraid of the dark?

2. How did his parents help him not to be afraid?

3. What did you think about a monster being afraid of people?

4. Where in the story did you think that Clyde was still afraid?

Think about how Clyde felt about the dark. How could you help him with his problem? What could you do to make him feel better? Write a story that tells how you could help Clyde Monster not to be afraid of the dark.

Bedtime

by Patricia Hubbell

Hop away
Skip away
Jump away
Leap!
Day is all crumpled
And lies in a heap.

Jump away
Skip away
Hop away
Creep!
Night comes and coaxes
The world to sleep.

Cause and Effect

Look at the picture. What is the dog doing? The dog is barking. Why is the dog barking? Someone is ringing the doorbell. A sentence that tells about the picture might be:

The dog is barking because someone is ringing the doorbell.

What is the dog in the picture doing? The dog is barking. This is *what happened,* or the **effect.**

Why is the dog barking? Someone is ringing the doorbell. This is the *reason why* something happened, or the **cause.**

Read this sentence:

Nick was sad because Robin moved away.

The sentence tells that Nick was sad. This is what happened, or the effect. The sentence also tells the reason why, or the cause, for Nick's being sad: Robin moved away.

Now read the following sentences. Find the cause and the effect in each sentence by asking what is happening and the reason why it is happening.

1. Sue turned on the light because the room was dark.
2. The room was dark, so Sue turned on the light.

Sometimes words like *because* and *so* help you to see what is happening and the reason why it is happening. Look for these words as you read.

The sun is far away from our planet, Earth. How does the sun help our planet?

Sun Up, Sun Down

by Gail Gibbons

The sun wakes me up. It comes up in the east and shines in my window. It lights up my room. It makes my room warm. It colors the clouds and the sky. I get up and get dressed.

My mother calls me. She wants me
to eat my cereal. It is made from
whole wheat. My dad tells me the sun
helps the wheat grow. He says the sun
helps plants and trees grow big and tall.

While I'm eating my cereal, I ask my parents a question: "How far away is the sun?" My mother tells me it is very far away from our planet, Earth. She says that the sun is a very big star. It looks bigger than the other stars because it is nearer to Earth than other stars are.

My dad says the sun keeps our planet warm. He says Earth would be dark and cold if there were no sun. Nothing could live on Earth without the sun.

My dad also tells me that the sun will shine on the other side of our planet while I'm sleeping. He says that Earth spins as it moves around the sun. It makes one full spin every day.

When the side of the planet Earth we live on faces the sun, it is day. When our side is turned away from the sun, it is night. At night, the sky is dark. It is time to sleep.

1. How does the sun help people and plants on Earth?

2. How important is the sun to people on Earth?

3. When did you first learn that the sun is a very big star?

4. What did you read that helps you know that the earth turns?

You have just read about some of the things the sun does. Think about three things the sun does for us. Write a story about three ways the sun helps us.

What does Caroline Porcupine have to do to get a new job on the Claws and Paws newspaper? Do you think she will get the job? Why?

Forecast

by Malcolm Hall

Stan Groundhog stood up. The whole party was for him. After many years, Stan was going away. He was leaving his job as weather forecaster for the *Claws and Paws* newspaper.

Theodore Cat, who was the owner of the paper, said, "Stan, give us your last weather forecast."

"All right," said Stan. He went to the window and looked outside. Next he looked down at his shadow. Then he said, "It will be warm and sunny all afternoon. It won't rain. Now I have to be going. Thanks for the party."

With that, there was a crack of lightning. All the lights in the office went out. Next came the thunder. Ka—ka—kabloom!!! Then the rain started to come down.

Stan waved good-bye and left.

Theodore looked around the room. "Does anyone know a groundhog who needs a job?"

Caroline Porcupine asked, "Does the forecaster have to be a groundhog?"

"Yes," said Theodore. "Everyone knows that groundhogs know when spring is coming by looking at their shadows. That's why I want another groundhog as a weather forecaster."

Caroline said, "I want the job. You see, I know a lot about the weather. Last year, I took a class in weather forecasting."

"Is that so?" said Theodore.

"Yes it is," said Caroline right back. "I can make real forecasts. If you let me, I will show you."

"All right," said Theodore. "Let's make a bet. You forecast the weather for all of next week. If you are right five days in a row, I will give you the job. If not, I'll get a groundhog."

"Theodore, I'll take your bet," said Caroline.

The next day, Caroline took her weather instruments to work. She had instruments for all kinds of things.

All that morning, Caroline set up her instruments. One by one, the animals stopped working. They walked over to Caroline's desk and watched her. By afternoon she was ready. She wrote down everything that her instruments told her.

Then Caroline looked up. "I am ready to make my forecast for the week. Today is Monday. It will be nice for the rest of the day. Tuesday, it will be sunny and warm. Wednesday, it will be cold. Thursday, it will rain." The animals looked at each other and smiled. So far, the forecast seemed good—maybe Caroline would be right!

Caroline went on, "On Friday, it will be cold in the morning, with snow in the afternoon." The animals were surprised.

Theodore laughed. "Snow? Did you
say snow? Caroline, look outside.
The sky is bright blue, and it's been
very hot for weeks and weeks."

Caroline answered, "My instruments
say it will snow on Friday."

"All right," said Theodore. "If it
snows on Friday, you will get the job.
I'm going to keep on looking for a
groundhog, however."

On Thursday it rained the whole day.
Theodore came in very wet. He thought,
"Caroline's been right four days in a
row. Maybe I should give her the job
even if it doesn't snow on Friday."

Friday started out cold, just as Caroline had said it would. By noon, however, there was still no snow.

Theodore sat in his office, looking out the window. If he had turned his head, he would have seen Frank Beaver and Oscar Raccoon run past his door. Each one had a large sack. They were headed for the roof.

A little later, Theodore looked
outside. A white flake had just floated
down past his window! Then came
another flake . . . and another . . . and
another! He jumped up. "Snow! It's
really snowing!" he shouted.

Theodore ran out of his office.
"Caroline! It's snowing! You are the
greatest forecaster ever! I take back
everything I said."

Theodore was so happy that he just
about hugged Caroline. You never hug a
porcupine, however. So he took Caroline
into his office. "See! Look out the
window. It is snowing!" he said.

Caroline looked outside. "That doesn't look like snow to me," she said.

"Yes, it is," said Theodore. He opened the window. Flakes started to come in. One landed on his nose. "Aaaa—choo!!!" Theodore looked very surprised.

"Let me see that snowflake." He took the flake and held it up to the light. "I thought so. This is a feather!"

Theodore looked up on the roof. He saw Frank and Oscar holding sacks that had feathers in them.

"Come down from there!" shouted
Theodore. "Come into my office."

In Theodore's office, a little later,
the animals all looked out the window.
Flakes were coming down again. This
time it was *really* snowing.

"That's *real* snow!" said Theodore.

"Yes, it is!" said Caroline. "I told
you it would snow."

1. What did Caroline have to do to get the job of weather forecaster?
2. How did Caroline predict the weather?
3. What part of the story did you think was the funniest? Why?
4. Where in the story did you know what the animals thought about Caroline's Friday forecast?

Think and Write

Think about when Theodore almost hugged Caroline. Write a paragraph that tells what would have happened if Theodore really had hugged her.

Change in the Weather

by Ilo Orleans

I think it would be very good
To have some snow and sleet
In summer when
We need it most
To drive away the heat.

Maps

Maps are used to show many things. Street maps show you how to find your way around your town. Weather maps show you what the weather forecast is for many places.

If you know what the weather forecast is, you can plan your day. You will know to take an umbrella if the weather map shows that it is going to rain where you live. Because the weather changes every day, weather maps also change every day.

Look at the weather map on the next page. It shows what the weather forecast is for one day in the United States.

Below the map is the **legend,** or key, for the map. The legend helps you read the map. Each picture in the legend stands for something. The word next to each picture tells what that picture means.

By looking at the legend and the weather map, you can see what the weather forecast is for one day in the United States.

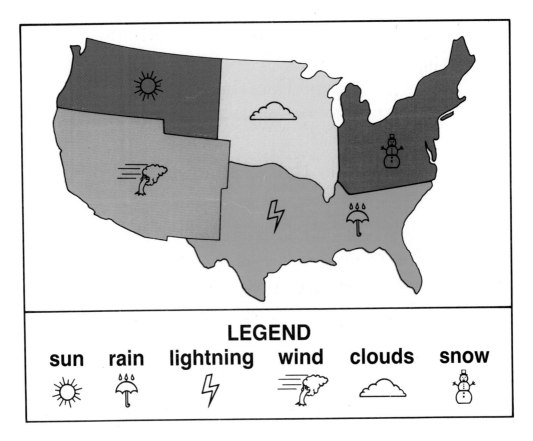

LEGEND

| sun | rain | lightning | wind | clouds | snow |

Use the legend to help you read the map on the next page. What is the weather in the blue zone? It is sunny. How do you know this? There is a sun in the blue zone on the map. What is the weather in the red zone? It is snowing. How do you know this? There is a snowman in the red zone on the map.

Read the following questions about the weather map. Use the map and the legend to help you answer the questions.

1. What is the weather in the yellow zone?
2. What is the weather in the green zone?
3. What is the weather in the orange zone?

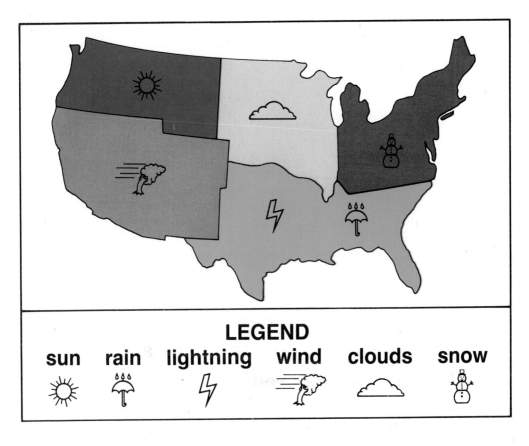

LEGEND

sun	rain	lightning	wind	clouds	snow

Remember, the legend of a map helps you read the map. Each picture stands for something that is on the map. By looking at the map and the map legend, you will know the weather forecast.

Raindrops fall from clouds in the sky. What happens to a raindrop after it falls to the ground?

Splash

by Ronda Maseman

This is the story of a raindrop. The raindrop's name is Splash.

Splash slides down the trunk of a tree. It lands on a little plant at the bottom of the tree. Splash slips down a leaf. It goes into a little pool made by many other raindrops.

Splash sinks into the ground, under
little roots, and slides around some rocks.
Splash stops. It rests on one of the big
tree roots. Then it is pulled inside the
root. Pop! Slowly Splash goes up the
root. Then Splash moves up through
all parts of the tree. Splash helps to
feed the tree.

At the top of the tree, Splash turns
into a gas and goes back to the clouds.
In the clouds, Splash becomes a
raindrop. Splash rests in a cloud for
a while.

Other raindrops come up to the cloud, too. Soon there are lots of raindrops in the cloud.

This time the cloud goes over a mountain. It is very cold on top of the mountain. The water in the cloud freezes and turns into ice and snow. Now Splash becomes a very pretty snowflake. Splash and the other snowflakes fall on top of the mountain.

The hot sun melts the snow. The melted snow and Splash then slide down the mountain. Splash and the melted snow turn into a little brook. The brook gets larger and larger and moves into a river.

By now some of the other raindrops in the river have turned back into a gas. They go up to the clouds while Splash is still having fun floating around in the big river.

Splash moves on down the river to the waterworks to be cleaned. After the water is cleaned, Splash and the water are sent through pipes to people's homes to be used.

Splash goes into a house and is pushed out through a long hose. This hose is being used to water the flowers. Now Splash falls onto one of the flowers. The sun gets hotter and hotter, and Splash turns into a gas. Soon Splash goes up into a cloud to come down as rain another day.

1. What happens to Splash after it falls from the first cloud?

2. How does Splash help the tree?

3. Tell three things that happen to Splash after it becomes a snowflake.

4. How do you know that Splash will not stay up in the cloud?

Think about the last time it rained. Write a story that tells some of the places where rain falls and what happens to the rain.

Owl does not want the moon to follow him home from the seashore. Does Owl change his mind?

Owl and the Moon

story and pictures by Arnold Lobel

One night, Owl went down to the seashore. He sat on a large rock and looked out at the waves. Everything was dark. Then a small tip of the moon came up over the edge of the sea.

Owl watched the moon. It climbed higher and higher into the sky. Soon the whole, round moon was shining.

Owl sat on the rock and looked up at the moon for a long time.

"If I am looking at you, moon, then you must be looking back at me. We must be very good friends."

The moon did not answer, but Owl said, "I will come back and see you again, moon. But now I must go home."

Owl walked down the path. He looked up at the sky. The moon was still there. It was following him.

"No, no, moon," said Owl. "It is kind of you to light my way. But you must stay up over the sea where you look so fine."

Owl walked on a little farther. He looked at the sky again. There was the moon coming right along with him.

"Dear moon," said Owl, "you really must not come home with me. My house is small. You would not fit through the door. And I have nothing to give you for supper."

Owl kept on walking. The moon sailed after him over the tops of the trees.

"Moon," said Owl, "I think that you do not hear me."

Owl climbed to the top of a hill. He shouted as loudly as he could, "Good-bye, moon!"

The moon went behind some clouds. Owl looked and looked. The moon was gone.

"It is always a little sad to say good-bye to a friend," said Owl.

Owl came home. He put on his pajamas and went to bed. The room was very dark. Owl was still feeling sad.

All at once, Owl's bedroom was filled
with silver light.

Owl looked out of the window. The
moon was coming from behind the clouds.

"Moon, you have followed me all the
way home. What a good, round friend you
are!" said Owl. Then Owl put his head on
the pillow and closed his eyes.

The moon was shining down through the
window. Owl did not feel sad at all.

1. Why didn't Owl want the moon to follow him home? Did he change his mind?
2. Why did Owl think the moon was following him home?
3. What did Owl think when the moon went behind the cloud?
4. When did you find out that the moon really had followed Owl home?

Think

and

Write

Owl and the moon were good friends. Think about what makes a good friend. Write a story that tells about something you and a good friend could do together.

Long ago, people made up this story to tell why there is day and night. What promise did the sun make? Why?

How the Sun Made a Promise and Kept It

*A Canadian Indian myth
retold by Margery Bernstein
and Janet Kobrin*

Long, long ago, there were rivers and lakes. There was dry land.

Sometimes Earth was a beautiful place for people to live. Other times, however, it was not a good place to live. In those days, the sun went wherever it wanted to go. It didn't always come near Earth. When the sun was away, Earth was dark and cold.

One of the people who lived then and who thought about Earth was named Weese-ke-jak. "I must do something," he said. "We need the sun for light and to warm us."

Weese-ke-jak thought and thought. At last he had an idea.

"The next time the sun comes near Earth," Weese-ke-jak thought, "I will catch it in a net. I will keep it close to Earth. Then Earth will always be warm and light."

Weese-ke-jak made a net out of ropes. The net was very large. Then Weese-ke-jak waited.

When the sun came near Earth
again, Weese-ke-jak took his net. He
swung it around and around. Then he
threw it up into the sky. The net
dropped over the sun. The sun was
trapped!

Weese-ke-jak pulled the net with the
sun in it down to Earth. He tied the
ropes to a tree stump.

The sun pulled and pulled. It could
not get itself free. "Weese-ke-jak, let me
go," begged the sun. "Let me go! Why
do you keep me in this net?"

"I have trapped you so that I can
keep you near Earth," answered
Weese-ke-jak. "Now Earth will be
warm and light all the time."

Weese-ke-jak would not let the sun
go. He had pulled the sun too near
Earth, however. It began to get hotter
and hotter.

Soon it was so hot that the birds
flew down out of the sky to see what
had happened. The animals came out of
the forests.

"If it gets any hotter," thought Weese-ke-jak, "everything will burn. I must let the sun out of the net. Maybe I can make the sun promise not to go too far away."

Then Weese-ke-jak called to the sun. "I might let you go, but you must promise something first."

"I will promise anything you say, Weese-ke-jak," answered the sun. "Just let me go."

"Well . . ." said Weese-ke-jak, "will you keep your promise?"

"I will keep my promise," cried the sun. "What must I do?"

"You must never go too far away," said Weese-ke-jak. "You may come close to the edges of Earth, but only in the morning and at night. In the daytime, you must come just near enough to warm Earth."

"I will do as you say," said the sun. "Now, please let me go!"

Weese-ke-jak went over to free the sun. The sun was so hot that he could not get near the net.

So Weese-ke-jak called to the animals. "I cannot get close to the sun," he said. "Can anyone help me?"

A few of the animals were brave.
They tried to help Weese-ke-jak.

First, Deer tried to free the sun.
Then Fox tried. Then Otter tried. They
could not get near enough. The sun was
too hot.

Then Beaver said, "I will try." In
those days, Beaver did not look the
same as he looks now. He had only a
few small teeth. His fur was rough. He
was not very beautiful, but he was very
brave.

Beaver ran to the net. He began to
bite the tough ropes that held the net.
The sun was very, very hot, but Beaver
did not give up.

At last, Beaver bit through the tough rope. The sun was free! It rose up from Earth like a balloon.

Earth became cooler. Weese-ke-jak and the animals were happy. They ran to thank Beaver.

Beaver, however, was not happy. The heat from the sun had burned his coat. He had very little fur left.

Weese-ke-jak said, "Don't be sad, Beaver. Because you were so brave, I will give you two presents."

Weese-ke-jak gave Beaver a beautiful new fur coat. He gave Beaver a new set of fine, sharp teeth.

Weese-ke-jak did not put any fur on Beaver's tail. "Beaver's tail will never have any fur," said Weese-ke-jak, "so everyone will remember how brave he was. They will remember that he set the sun free."

The sun remembered, too. And in all the days of the world since then, the sun has kept this promise.

1. What promise did the sun make? Why?

2. Why did Weese-ke-jak throw a net around the sun?

3. What did Beaver do to help?

4. How did you know that catching the sun was not a good idea?

What would happen if the sun shone all the time? Would the grass dry up and die? Would people get sunburned? Write two sentences that tell other things that could happen if the sun shone all the time.

Thinking About "Earth and Sky"

In "Earth and Sky," you read about many ways that the earth and sky help each other. You learned that the sun gives the earth light and makes it warm. You learned about what happens to a raindrop after it falls from the sky. You read about Owl and how he made friends with the moon.

The earth and sky help each other in many ways. What other new and surprising things did you learn about the earth and the sky? What other things would you like to know about how the earth and sky work together?

1. Why would Clyde Monster have been happy if the moon had followed him home?

2. Would Theodore have needed Caroline to forecast the weather if the sun had stayed up in the sky all the time? Why?

3. How might the sun and a raindrop like Splash help wheat grow?

4. How are Frank Beaver in "Forecast" and Beaver in "How the Sun Made a Promise and Kept It" alike?

Read on Your Own

Small Cloud by Ariane. Dutton. This is a
   tale about how rain is made. The
   beautiful pictures help tell the story.

Happy Birthday, Moon by Frank Asch.
   Prentice-Hall. When a bear finds out that
   he and Moon have the same birthday,
   he gives Moon a hat as a present.

Moongame by Frank Asch. Prentice-Hall.
   Bear is playing hide-and-seek with
   Moon.

The Way to Start a Day by Byrd Baylor.
   Scribner's. This book tells how people
   around the world greet the day and how
   people did it long ago.

What Makes It Rain? by Keith Brandt. Troll.
   This book follows a raindrop as it moves
   from one place to another.

Rain and Hail by Franklyn Branley. Harper. This book tells how rain and hail are made.

A January Fog Will Freeze a Hog and Other Weather Folklore by Hubert Davis. Crown. This book tells how sayings about the weather got started.

Wake Up, Jeremiah by Ronald Himler. Harper. A young boy wakes up to see the sun come up. He goes to a special place to watch it.

All Wet! All Wet! by James Skofield. Harper. A boy goes for a walk in the rain. He discovers the sights, smells, and sounds on a day when it rains.

Kaleidoscopes

Have you ever seen a kaleidoscope? Kaleidoscopes have tiny bits of colored glass at the end of a long tube. As you turn the tube, the colors change and make pictures. The pictures in a kaleidoscope are always changing. In "Kaleidoscopes," you will read about many things and people who change.

The people in "Kaleidoscopes" find that things are not what they seem to be. As you read "Kaleidoscopes," think about the changes that take place in each story.

How do three days in the library change Beatrice? What doesn't change?

Beatrice Doesn't Want To

by Laura Joffe Numeroff

Beatrice didn't like books. She didn't even like to read. More than that, she hated going to the library. But that's where her brother Henry had to take her three afternoons in a row.

Henry had to do a report on dinosaurs. Henry also had to look after Beatrice.

"Why don't you get some books?"
Henry said when they got to the library.

"I don't want to," Beatrice said.

"Look at how many books there are!"
Henry tried.

"I don't want to," Beatrice said again.

"Then what do you want to do?"
Henry asked her.

"I want to watch you," she said.

"I have to work," said Henry.

"I'll watch until you're finished," she
said.

"I give up," Henry said.

Henry worked on his report. Beatrice sat in a chair and watched him. Henry tried not to notice her.

The second day, Beatrice didn't even want to go inside. "Come on, Bea," Henry said.

"I don't want to," Beatrice told him.

"I have to work," said Henry.

"I just want to sit outside," Beatrice answered.

"All right," said Henry, "but don't move until I come out." Beatrice promised. Henry went inside to do his report.

Suddenly Henry felt drops of water.
He didn't know where they were coming
from. Then he felt someone tap his
shoulder. Henry turned around, and
there was Beatrice. She was soaking wet.
"It's raining," she said.

"I give up," said Henry.

It was still raining the third day.
Beatrice had to go inside this time. She
followed Henry around while he looked
for more books.

"Can I hold some?" Beatrice asked.

Henry gave her some books to hold.

"They're too heavy!" Beatrice yelled. Suddenly the heavy books dropped onto her foot, and she began to cry.

"I really do give up!" said Henry. "Look, Bea, I've got to finish this report. Please!" Henry begged her.

"Henry," said Beatrice, "could I have some water?"

They went down a hall to look for some water. Suddenly Henry saw a sign. This was it!

The librarian
will read

"Alfred Mouse Has a
Brand New House"
today
in the children's room
4:00

"Come on," said Henry.

"I don't want to," Beatrice said.

"That's too bad!" shouted Henry.

Before she knew it, Beatrice was in a room full of boys and girls. Henry walked out just as she started to say, "I don't want . . ."

"Hello. My name is Wanda. This is the second time I've heard this story," said the girl in the next chair.

"Big deal!" said Beatrice.

"Alfred Mouse lived in a brand new house," the librarian began to read. She held the book up so everyone could see the pictures. Beatrice looked out the window.

"Alfred Mouse also had new skates," the librarian went on.

Beatrice loved to skate. She looked at the librarian. "But Alfred's mother wasn't too happy when he skated through the house," the librarian read.

The boys and girls laughed.

Beatrice smiled. She thought about the time she had tried skating in her own house. Then Beatrice laughed. She listened to the whole story.

When the story was over, Beatrice went up to the librarian. "May I see that book, please?" she asked.

"Yes," said the librarian. Beatrice sat down in a chair and looked at each picture over and over. Suddenly she felt someone tapping her shoulder.

"Time to go," Henry said in her ear.

Beatrice kept looking at the pictures and didn't notice him. Henry put Beatrice's hat on her head. "We have to go home now," he said.

Beatrice kept on looking at the pictures.

"Come on, Bea," Henry said.

"I don't want to," Beatrice told him.

1. How did Beatrice change on the last day in the library?

2. How did Beatrice stay the same from beginning to end?

3. How did Henry finally get to do his report on dinosaurs?

4. What words in the story tell that Henry needed help with Beatrice?

Beatrice changed her mind when she found a book she liked. Have you ever changed your mind about something? Write a paragraph that tells what you didn't like and how you changed.

*A prince wants to change his life.
He thinks he will be happier living
a simpler life. What does the prince
find out?*

The Simple Prince

adapted from a book by Jane Yolen

There was once a prince who wanted
to live a simple life. So he clapped his
hands three times to call his servants.

"Bring me some simple clothes," he
yelled. "I am going out into the world
to live the simple life." So the servants
found a plain suit and a plain hat as well.

The prince clapped his hands three
times and told his servants to bring him
a simple picnic lunch to eat on his way.
Then he rode for a long time. At last, he
came to the house of a simple farmer.

The prince got off his horse and went
to the door. He clapped his hands three
times. Nothing happened. He tapped his
foot. Then he shouted, "Open up!" The
door was opened. The farmer looked out.

"I have come to live the simple life,"
said the prince. He walked inside.

The farmer looked at his wife. She
looked at the prince. The prince did not
notice. He sat down on a chair and
clapped his hands three times. "I want
some cheese and a cup of tea," the
prince said.

The farmer looked at his wife. She
shook her head. The farmer just smiled.

The farmer cut the prince some cheese.
Then the farmer said: "Cheese and tea.
That is simple. Here is the cheese. As for
the tea, we need fire and water. First I
must saw the wood for the fire. It is
simple. Come with me."

The prince went outside with the farmer.
They found some wood. They sawed and
they sawed and they sawed some more. At
last the prince cried out, "Enough! Enough!
I can do no more."

"We are done," said the farmer. He filled the prince's arms with wood and led him back to the house. Then the farmer made the fire. The prince sat down again.

"Now it is time to get the water," said the farmer's wife. "It is simple. Come with me."

So the prince followed the farmer's wife to the well. Arm over arm, he pulled the pail up. He poured the water from the pail into a pitcher. Then he pulled up more pails of water. He poured the water into three pitchers. At last the prince cried: "Enough! Enough! I can do no more."

"We are done," said the farmer's wife.
She gave the prince a pitcher for each
hand. She put one on his head, too. Then
she led him back to the house.

The farmer's wife put the water into
a pot and put the pot on the fire. When
it was hot, she made tea. But the prince
had worked so hard, he was two times as
hungry as before. He clapped his hands
three times and said, "Bring me some
bread and butter with my tea."

"That is simple enough," said the farmer. "But butter comes from milk, and milk comes from a cow. Come with me."

So the prince followed the farmer to the cow. There the prince held the pail while the farmer milked the cow. The cow's tail hit the prince's face. The cow's feet kicked the prince's legs. At last the prince cried, "Enough! Enough! I can do no more."

"It is done," said the farmer.

Back in the house, the farmer made the prince churn, and churn, and churn the milk into butter. When the butter was finished, the prince fell back on the chair. He clapped his hands three times. "My butter needs some bread," he said.

"That is simple," said the farmer's wife. "But first we must bake it. Come with me to help."

So she gave the prince some dough. He patted the dough. He pushed the dough. He pulled the dough. He punched the dough. At last the prince cried, "Enough! Enough! I can do no more."

"It's done," said the farmer's wife.
Then she baked the dough.

The prince was so tired from all his
simple work that he went to sleep. He slept
through the bread-baking and supper. He
woke up the next morning. He felt very
tired. He tried to clap his hands—one
time, two times, three times. His hands
hurt from all the work he had done.

"Please," he asked, "may I have
something to eat?"

"It's simple," the farmer's wife said.
Before she could finish, the prince
jumped up from the chair.

"Enough! Enough!" he cried. "I can live
no more of the simple life. It is much too
hard for me!"

The prince ran out the door, climbed on
his horse, and raced back home as fast as
he could go. His servants helped him off
his horse, and the prince said, "Thank you."

Then he really wanted something to eat. So he asked, "Please, may I have some bread and butter."

His servants were happy to be asked so nicely. They went quickly to get the bread and butter and a pitcher of milk.

From that day to this, the prince lived happily. He never again clapped his hands for anything. He was always careful to say "please" and "thank you." It was so much simpler that way.

1. Was the prince happier living a simple life? Why?

2. What did the prince learn about life on a farm?

3. How did the prince learn about the simple life?

4. What made you think that the prince learned his lesson?

The prince learned to say "please" and "thank you." Think about some reasons for being nice. Write a paragraph that tells three reasons why it is a good idea to be nice.

153

Politeness

by A. A. Milne

If people ask me,
I always tell them:
"Quite well, thank you. I'm very glad to say."
If people ask me,
I always answer,
"Quite well, thank you, how are you today?"
I always answer,
I always tell them,
If they ask me,
Politely. . . .
BUT SOMETIMES
  I wish
    That they wouldn't.

Jenny's father wants to teach her how to play tennis, but Jenny has different ideas. How does Jenny show her father what she really wants to do?

Jenny and the Tennis Nut

by Janet Schulman

Jenny stood on her hands. Just then her father came into the room. "Look at me, it is my best handstand yet," she said.

"What's so great about it?" asked her father.

She looked at him upside down and said, "I have been standing like this for a minute."

"Well, I have been standing like this for much longer," said her father. "Get yourself right side up. I have a surprise."

He gave her a long box. "It's a tennis racket," Jenny said.

"I'm going to teach you tennis and this will be your racket," he said.

Jenny picked up the racket. "What if I don't like tennis?" she asked.

"You're going to love tennis. I love tennis. Your mother does, and you will, too," said her father.

Her father picked up his racket and some tennis balls. "Come on outside, Jenny. We can hit the ball," he said.

He drew a line across the wall. "This line is the top of the net," he said.

"Some net. I can't jump over it when I win," said Jenny.

"First things first, Jenny. First learn to hit the ball. Like this," he said. Thonk went the ball. He hit the ball again and again. He loved hitting a tennis ball so much that he forgot about teaching Jenny.

Jenny did not mind. She was doing cartwheels on the grass.

At last he stopped. "Now you try," he said. He threw a ball to her. Swish went her racket. "Keep your eye on the ball, and you won't miss," he said. He threw another ball to her.

She kept her eye on the ball. Zing went the ball over the fence and into Mrs. Wister's yard.

"I'll get the ball," said Jenny. She took a running start and jumped up, up and over Mrs. Wister's fence.

"That was pretty good," said her father. Jenny smiled. "Oh, I can jump a lot higher than that," she said.

"I meant that you hit the ball pretty well," he said.

"Oh," she said. Jenny jumped back over the fence. "Then why did it go the wrong way into Mrs. Wister's yard?"

"Because you were facing the wall—I mean the net. Always stand with your side to the net," he said.

Jenny made a face.

"You will learn," he said. He threw a ball to her. She kept her eye on the ball. She stood with her side to the net. She swung the racket. Thonk went the ball.

"That's perfect!" said her father.

"Oh, Daddy, stop kidding," she said.

"Don't you want to be a great tennis player?" he asked.

"No. I want to be a great circus acrobat," she said.

"A circus acrobat! There are not many circuses looking for acrobats these days. You can play tennis anywhere. Think what fun we will have!" he said.

"You mean think what fun you will have," she said.

"Oh, Jenny," he said. "I just want you to have a sport you can do well and enjoy. That's why I want to teach you tennis."

She shook her head sadly. "Oh, Daddy, you have a one-track mind. Tennis, tennis, tennis," she said. "You are a tennis nut. I already have a sport I can do well, and I enjoy. Look!" She did four perfect cartwheels. Then she did a handstand and a flip.

Her father watched her. His eyes were wide open. "Hey, that's good. You are wonderful, Jenny."

Jenny ran to her father and threw her arms around him. "You mean it's all right for me to do my tricks?" she asked.

"It's more than all right. I want you to. I am going to put up some rings and a bar with a nice soft mat under them," he said. "You do gymnastics well and you really enjoy it. Gymnastics is right for you."

"Just like tennis is right for you. Right?" she said.

"Right!" he answered. They were both happy.

Jenny looked up at her father. "There is something else, Daddy. Can I take gymnastics classes?"

Her father laughed. "You can read minds, too. Maybe you do belong in a circus," he said.

Jenny ran to the house. "I am going to tell Mom what my game is," she said.

Her father picked up his racket and a ball. There was no question what his game was.

In a few minutes Jenny came out again. She did a flip and watched her father hit the ball.

At last he stopped. "Maybe when you are older you will want a second game," he said. "I'll always be ready to teach you tennis when you are ready to learn."

"Okay," said Jenny. "If you ever want a second game, I'll always be ready to teach you cartwheels and flips. You would love it." She grinned at him, upside down.

1. How does Jenny show her father what she really wants to do?

2. Why doesn't Jenny want to learn how to play tennis?

3. How was the problem solved?

4. Where in the story did you first begin to think that Jenny would not have to learn to play tennis?

Think

and

Write

Think about the tricks a circus acrobat does. Write three or four sentences that tell about things a circus acrobat must be able to do well.

Main Idea and Details

As you read a paragraph, think about what the paragraph tells you. Often, one sentence tells you what the whole paragraph is about. That sentence is the **main idea.** Other sentences in the paragraph tell you more about the main idea. Those sentences give you **details.**

Read the following paragraph.

Dogs can do many kinds of work. They pull sleds. They take care of cows. Dogs can even lead blind people.

What is the main idea of the paragraph? The main idea is that dogs can do many kinds of work.

What are the details in the paragraph? The details are that dogs pull sleds, they take care of cows, and they can even lead blind people.

Now read the following paragraph.

Our class is going to put on a play with four people in it. Carla will be the wise owl who lives in the forest. Robert will be the friendly elephant. Kim is going to be the ugly monster. Rick will be the king who chases the monster away.

What is the main idea of this paragraph? The main idea is that our class is going to put on a play with four people in it. What are four details?

The main idea tells about the paragraph. The details tell more about the main idea. Looking for main ideas and details in paragraphs will help you understand what you are reading.

There are many different animals on farms. Read to find out some details about each of these animals.

Farm Animals

by Grace Moremen

A farm is an interesting place to visit. Many animals live on the farm. You'll see cows, pigs, chickens, and horses on the farm. You'll hear the sounds these animals make. You'll learn why farm animals are important.

Before you get to the farm buildings, you can see the cows. They are standing behind a fence. Cows chew and chew with their mouths full. They brush flies away with their tails. You might hear the cows mooing.

The farmer raises some cows for meat. This meat is called beef.

The farmer also raises some cows for milk. These cows are milked in the barn. The farmer uses a machine to milk the cows. Maybe you can watch.

Near the barn is the pig pen. There you might hear the sounds of the pigs. You can see the mother pig with her many babies. Baby pigs are called piglets. The farmer raises pigs for meat. This meat is called pork.

The farmer's chickens may be inside the barn, or they may be running around the yard. Baby chickens are called chicks. You might hear the chickens clucking softly. Chickens give us eggs and meat.

Now you run to see the horses in the field. They watch you coming with their big eyes. Maybe the horses know you have carrots for them. When they see the carrots, the horses make little sounds.

Some of the horses have babies. A baby horse is called a foal. Foals like to jump and run. They are fun to watch.

Horses used to do a lot of work on the farm. Now the farmer has trucks and tractors to do this work. The farmer raises horses for people to ride.

At last your visit to the farm is over. You learned some details about farm animals. You learned why farm animals are important. You learned that cows, pigs, and chickens give us food. Horses give us rides. Most of all, you had fun watching the farm animals and listening to their sounds.

1. Why do farmers have different animals?

2. Why is a farm an interesting place?

3. Which farm animal do you like best? Why?

4. On what page did you find the name for a baby horse? What is the name?

Think about farm animals. Pretend you are going on a field trip. Write a paragraph telling where you might go and what you might see and learn.

Old MacDonald Had a Farm

an American folk song

1. Old MacDonald had a farm,
    e—i—e—i—o!
   And on this farm he had some pigs,
    e—i—e—i,—o!
   With an oink-oink here,
    and an oink-oink there.
   Here an oink, there an oink,
    everywhere an oink-oink.
   Old MacDonald had a farm,
    e—i—e—i—o!

2. And on this farm he had some cows,
   e—i—e—i—o!
With a moo-moo here,
   and a moo-moo there.
Here a moo, there a moo,
   everywhere a moo-moo.
Old MacDonald had a farm,
   e—i—e—i—o!

3. And on this farm he had some chickens,
   e—i—e—i—o!
With a cluck-cluck here,
   and a cluck-cluck there.
Here a cluck, there a cluck,
   everywhere a cluck-cluck.
Old MacDonald had a farm,
   e—i—e—i—o!

175

This is a play about a duckling who is very different from the other ducklings. He does not like to be different. Does he change his mind?

The Ugly Duckling

A fairy tale retold by Ruth Rogg

CHARACTERS

Narrator   **The Ugly Duckling**
Mother Duck   **All the Swans**

Narrator: It was a beautiful spring day in the country. The sun was warm. Down in the meadow, Mother Duck was sitting on five eggs that were ready to hatch.

Mother Duck: I think today will be the day my eggs will hatch. I can't wait to see my little ducklings. I know they will all be beautiful.

Narrator: Four eggs began to hatch.

Mother Duck: Oh, little ones, you are beautiful! I still have one big egg to sit on. Go play while I sit on this big egg.

Narrator: Mother Duck sat and sat. At last a sound came from the big egg. A big gray duckling came out of the egg.

Mother Duck: My, you are a big duckling! You are larger than your brothers and sisters.

Narrator: The big duckling looked at himself in the pond. He looked very different from his brothers and sisters. He was very sad about what he saw.

Mother Duck: You are mine. I love you even if you are different.

Narrator: Mother Duck took her five
ducklings for a swim. Mother Duck
was happy with her ducklings. They
could all swim so well.

When the animals in the meadow
saw the big gray duckling, they
always made fun of him. They
sometimes called him the Ugly
Duckling.

The animals were also mean to
the gray duckling. His sisters and
brothers were mean, too. They played
tricks on him and made fun of him.

The Ugly Duckling: I'm so ugly. I'll go away. No one likes me.

Narrator: The Ugly Duckling flew up over a tall tree. He went far away. He stopped in a marsh where wild geese lived. The geese were kind to him. The Ugly Duckling stayed with the geese for a long time.

The red and yellow leaves turned brown. They fell from the trees. The water in the marsh became cold. It started to freeze. Winter came. The cold winds blew. The Ugly Duckling had to swim fast to keep from freezing.

The Ugly Duckling: I am so cold. I must keep swimming. I am so sad.

Narrator: Winter went by. Spring came. Trees began to bloom. The sun began to shine again. The wind was soft. One day, the Ugly Duckling flew to a beautiful pond. He saw many swans there.

The Ugly Duckling: Oh, look at the beautiful white swans swimming in the pond! I wish they would play with me, but I know they won't. I am so ugly.

Narrator: The Ugly Duckling looked at himself in the water. He was very surprised! His gray feathers had turned white!

The Ugly Duckling: I am a swan!

All the Swans: Come swim with us. You are such a wonderful swan. We have never seen one so beautiful.

Narrator: Now the swan knew he was not an ugly duckling. He was a beautiful, happy swan.

1. Why did the duckling think he was different?

2. Why did he change his mind?

3. Why did the Ugly Duckling go away?

4. How do you feel about the geese in the story? Why?

5. What words in the story tell how Mother Duck felt about the Ugly Duckling?

Think about how you are different from everyone else and how that makes you special. Write a paragraph that tells what makes you a special person.

Caterpillars look very different from butterflies. How does a caterpillar change into a butterfly?

The Caterpillar's Surprise

by Grace Moremen

Some caterpillars turn into butterflies. Other caterpillars turn into moths. This is surprising because caterpillars look very different from butterflies or moths. Let's see how caterpillars turn into butterflies.

First, butterflies lay eggs on plants. The eggs are about as big as the head of a pin. Soon, caterpillars come out of the eggs. Little caterpillars look like tiny worms with many feet.

Some caterpillars have soft skin. Others have rough skin.

As a butterfly caterpillar grows, it becomes too big to fit inside its skin. So the old skin cracks open and falls off. Now the caterpillar has a new, bigger skin. The caterpillar will get a new skin three or four times while it is growing.

Butterfly caterpillars eat all day. Sometimes they eat all night, too. Caterpillars eat plants.

Some butterfly caterpillars will grow as long as a fingernail. Others will grow as big and fat as a crayon.

After a few weeks, the butterfly caterpillar stops eating. It finds a plant to hold on to and spins a covering around itself. The covering is called a *cocoon*. The caterpillar inside the cocoon is now called a *pupa*.

Inside the cocoon, the pupa is changing. It is growing legs and wings and a whole new body, but you cannot see this happening. It is becoming a butterfly.

Then one day the cocoon cracks open. The butterfly pushes out its head. It sticks up its two feelers. Then it wiggles its body out of the cocoon. The new butterfly stands up on its six thin legs.

The new butterfly is wet. Its wings are folded. Now the butterfly pumps liquid into its wings. This liquid helps the butterfly to open them. Then the butterfly dries its wings by flapping them. You can see how different the butterfly looks from the caterpillar.

A butterfly lays eggs. A baby caterpillar comes out of each egg. The caterpillar spins a cocoon and turns into a pupa. Then the pupa turns into a butterfly. This is the caterpillar's wonderful surprise.

1. How does a caterpillar become a butterfly?

2. Why does a butterfly caterpillar need to grow new skin?

3. How does the butterfly caterpillar get inside its cocoon?

4. Where on page 188 did you know about the caterpillar's surprise?

A caterpillar is different from the butterfly it becomes. How is a baby different from a grown-up? Write a paragraph that tells three ways babies are different from grown-ups.

Follow Directions
Make a Paper Caterpillar

You have just learned how a caterpillar turns into a butterfly. Now you can make a caterpillar to play with.

To make your caterpillar, you must follow the directions carefully. Here are some things to remember about following directions.

1. Get all the things you need together before you begin.
2. Read the steps very carefully.
3. Begin with step 1 and follow all the steps in order.
4. Do not leave out any steps.

Paper Chain Caterpillars

Things you will need:

a ruler | paste

scissors | crayons

1 sheet of yellow paper | string

1 sheet of green paper | a pencil

1. With a pencil and ruler, draw four 2-inch strips on the yellow paper.

Cut along the lines. Do the same with the green paper.

2.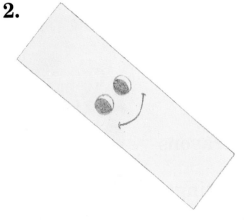

2. With a crayon, draw big eyes and a mouth on one yellow strip.

3. On one green strip, draw two feelers.

3.

4. Cut out the feelers. Paste them just over the eyes. Fold them so they stand straight up.

4.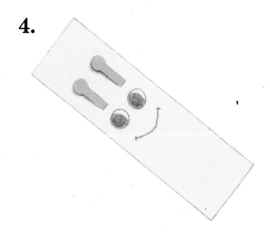

5. Take the head and make it into a circle. Paste the ends together.

5.

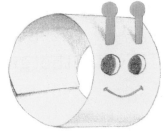

6. Now take a green strip and make it into a circle through the head of the caterpillar. You are making a paper chain.

7. Keep doing this until you have used all seven strips. Your caterpillar is finished.

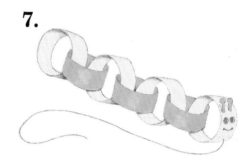

You may want to draw stripes or spots on your caterpillar. You can also tie a string to its head. Pull the string, and the caterpillar will follow you wherever you go!

Thinking About "Kaleidoscopes"

In "Kaleidoscopes," you read about many interesting changes. You found out that the prince really liked life in his castle better than working hard on a farm. The Ugly Duckling found out that he was really a beautiful swan. You learned how a caterpillar changed into a beautiful butterfly.

Most of these changes were fine at first, but some of the characters found that things are not always what they seem to be. What are some other changes that took place in the stories? What things didn't change?

1. How are Beatrice and the prince in "The Simple Prince" alike?

2. How are Jenny and Beatrice alike?

3. What are some of the jobs that have to be done on the farm in "The Simple Prince" and on the farm in "Farm Animals"?

4. How are the Ugly Duckling and caterpillars alike?

Read on Your Own

Farming Today — Yesterday's Way by Cheryl
W. Bellville. Carolrhoda. This book
shows you what a farm is like.

The Very Hungry Caterpillar by Eric Carle.
Putnam. A caterpillar is very, very
hungry and eats his way through all
kinds of food. At the end, he is ready
for a big change.

Chester's Barn by Lindee Climo. Tundra. In
this book you find out about all the
animals in Chester's barn. Each animal
has its own place and its own job.

The Animals of Buttercup Farm by Phoebe
and Judy Dunn. Random. This book tells
about what farm animals do and how
they are cared for.

Farm Babies by Russell Freedman. Holiday House. You will find out about many farm animals and how they look and act when they are very young.

Digger by Laura Joffe Numeroff. Dutton. A boy's father wants a dog. They can't have pets in their building. This book tells how they solve this problem.

The Year at Maple Hill Farm by Alice and Martin Provensen. Atheneum. This book tells how a farm changes through the year.

The Giants' Farm by Jane Yolen. Houghton Mifflin. A group of giants live together on a farm. This book has five stories about how they learn to get along.

Unit 4

Scrapbooks

A scrapbook is a book in which you put things that you would like to remember. In "Scrapbooks," you will read about some people who have made scrapbooks. You will also read about some special days that are fun to remember. See how people all over the world greet the new year. Read an old, old tale that has been told for many years about a small town.

As you read "Scrapbooks," think about the special times that the people in each story like to remember. What makes these times special?

Birdie Blue

Local Class
Visits City
Zoo

FIELD TRIP HUGE SUCCESS

Local Class
Visits City

This is a story about a boy who keeps
a scrapbook for his grandmother.
What does he put into the scrapbook?

Grandma Without Me

story and pictures by Judith Vigna

I don't want Thanksgiving this year.
It won't be any fun without Grandma.
Grandma is Dad's mother. She lives far
away, in another town.

I don't see why we can't visit
Grandma for Thanksgiving. We have to
stay home because Mom says things are
different now. Mom and Dad don't live
together anymore. Mom says I can visit
Dad's new house whenever I want.
That's great, but I want to visit
Grandma's house again. I like my room
there and the way Grandma fixes
pancakes for mc.

We've never had Thanksgiving without
Grandma. She always cooked a huge
turkey, and Mom and Dad and I put on
funny hats. One time I ate so much
turkey I got sick. It was the best day
of my life.

Now, Grandma and I write to each other all the time. A while ago, Grandma sent me a scrapbook and a letter. The letter said:

My darling boy,

Your mom doesn't want to visit me right now. Things will get better. It will just take time. One day we'll see each other again. I am sending a scrapbook for you to keep for us. Until we see each other again, we'll keep in touch through your scrapbook. I will always love you.

Grandma

The letter was the first thing I put into my scrapbook.

Grandma and I work on my scrapbook
a lot. I saved a purple leaf that I found,
and I put it into the scrapbook.

I put some other things into my
scrapbook. Grandma sent me a feather
from her bird's cage.

I took a picture of the new bike Dad
got me for my birthday.

Grandma sent me a funny picture she saw in the newspaper.

This morning I got a mailgram! It said:

```
             MAILGRAM

  Thanksgiving won't be the same
without my darling little boy.  I miss
  you.  Love and kisses from Grandma.
```

It was neat of Grandma to send me a
real mailgram for my scrapbook.
Grandma must really miss me! I think I'll
send her something special, so she won't
feel so bad.

I asked Mom for a really big sheet of paper. Then I asked her to help me. I told her that I wanted to lie down on the paper. She could draw around me. Then I could send the picture to Grandma. Grandma will feel like I'm at her house for Thanksgiving after all!

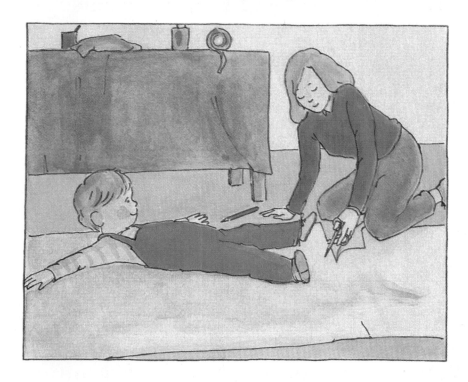

Mom has promised we can really go to visit Grandma next Thanksgiving.

1. What does the boy put into his scrapbook?

2. Why was the scrapbook a good idea?

3. What words in the story tell you the boy wants to do something special for his grandma?

In the story, the boy was sad because he could not be with his grandmother on Thanksgiving. Suppose you invited him to your house for Thanksgiving. Write a paragraph telling him what your Thanksgiving is like.

Keepsakes

by Leland B. Jacobs

I keep bottle caps,
I keep strings,
I keep keys and corks
And all such things.

When people say,
"What good are they?"
The answer's hard to get
For just how I will use them all
I don't know yet.

Classification

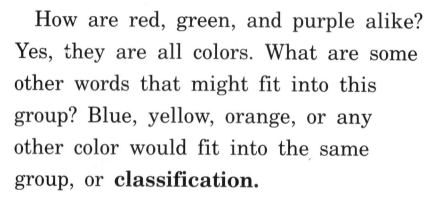

How are red, green, and purple alike? Yes, they are all colors. What are some other words that might fit into this group? Blue, yellow, orange, or any other color would fit into the same group, or **classification.**

How are chalk, a pen, and a pencil alike? They are all things that you write with. What are some other things that might fit into the same group? A crayon or anything else that you can write with would fit into the same group, or classification.

One way to group or **classify** things is to think about how they are the same.

210

Read the words on the left. Tell which word on the right would fit into the same group. Then tell why you picked that word.

1. truck
   bus

   van   tree   lake

2. walk
   run

   school   clock   hop

3. book
   pencil

   cat   paper   grass

4. sleep
   play

   house   peach   eat

When you want to classify things or put them into groups, you have to think about how the things are the same. There are different ways of putting things together. As you read the next selection, look for some ways that people classify things.

211

Making a scrapbook can be a lot of fun. What kinds of things can you put into a scrapbook?

Scrapbooks

by Alma Marshak Whitney

Have you ever thought of making a scrapbook? You can make a scrapbook about anything you want. The first thing you need is a book with blank pages. The book becomes a scrapbook when you start to put things into it.

Lisa Bates, Jason Cook, and Terry Parks are making scrapbooks. Lisa is making a scrapbook with pictures she collects. The name of her scrapbook is *The Lions*. The pictures are of the players on the Lions baseball team.

Lisa looks through newspapers for pictures of her favorite players on the Lions. Lisa cuts out the pictures she finds. Then she pastes these pictures into her scrapbook. Sometimes Lisa gets baseball cards with pictures of her favorite players on them. Lisa pastes these cards into her scrapbook, too.

Terry is making a scrapbook about the birthday party she had a few weeks ago. The name of her scrapbook is *My Favorite Birthday*.

Terry has put many things into her scrapbook. There is a list of her friends who came to the party. There is a list of the games they played. There is a balloon Terry let the air out of when the party was over. There are also the birthday cards Terry got from her friends at the party.

Terry is glad that she is making this scrapbook. She thinks it will help her remember how nice her birthday party was.

Jason is making a scrapbook he calls *My Book of Trips*. He plans to put into it things he collects from trips he takes.

Jason started making the scrapbook after he came home from visiting with his Aunt Betty and Uncle Mike. There is a ticket to a movie Jason saw with his aunt and uncle. There is a picture from a place where he ate lunch with them one day. There is a page from a newspaper that people read in the town where Aunt Betty and Uncle Mike live. There are cards with pictures of buildings Jason saw in the town. Jason even saved his airplane ticket to put into his scrapbook.

Jason likes to look at his scrapbook. It helps him remember what a good time he had on his trip. He wants to collect things from other trips. Then his scrapbook will help him remember the good times he has had on many trips.

Perhaps you might like to make a scrapbook. You can make a scrapbook about many different things. The things you put into your scrapbook will make it special to you.

1. What kinds of things can be put into a scrapbook?

2. Why might you keep a scrapbook?

3. Which scrapbook in the story did you like best? Why?

4. What words in the story tell why Terry keeps a scrapbook?

Think about something special you want to remember. Pretend you are going to make a scrapbook about that time. Write a paragraph that tells what your scrapbook will be about and three things you will put into it.

Wei Chou's family is getting ready for a special celebration. What does Wei Chou do to make the celebration really special?

The Year of the Smile

by John Yeates

Wei Chou was very happy today. It was the first day of the Chinese New Year. This morning Wei Chou's parents gave her a red envelope. There was money inside. It was a New Year's gift.

Wei Chou's real name was Susie. One day her father called her Wei Chou—which means "a smile" in Chinese. Wei Chou liked both names, but most of the time she used her Chinese name.

Wei Chou and her mother were making the house pretty. Over each doorway they placed a long, red silk ribbon. In each window they hung a red paper lantern. Wei Chou even tied a red ribbon around her puppy's neck.

"Red makes me happy," said Wei Chou.

"Good," said her mother. "Many things make you happy. That is why your father named you Wei Chou."

Wei Chou went into her room and hung the last lantern over her puppy's bed. Then she sat down near the puppy.

She thought of all the good things about the New Year's celebration. It was a happy time for the family. They got new clothes. They ate special foods. Wei Chou liked the Eight Treasure Dessert. Her mother and father made it every year. Sometimes they let her help.

Suddenly the puppy jumped from his
bed. He ran to the front door. Wei Chou
followed him. Her mother went to the
door, too.

"Why is the puppy barking so much?"
asked Wei Chou.

"He may know that we have a surprise
for you," said her mother. "I think I
hear the surprise now."

The front door opened. Wei Chou's
father came in. Someone was with him.

"It's Uncle Li!" shouted Wei Chou, as
she ran to meet him.

Uncle Li handed Wei Chou a box. When she opened it, she saw a beautiful doll. It was dressed in a Chinese costume. Wei Chou hugged her uncle and thanked him for the doll.

He said, "It was a long ride on the bus, but I wanted to help with the celebration. What time does the parade begin this afternoon?"

"We will not have a parade," said Wei Chou's father.

Uncle Li shook his head. He looked very sad. "No parade?" he asked.

"Not this year," said Wei Chou's father. "Mr. Wu always made plans for our parade, but he moved away."

Uncle Li did not smile for the rest of the morning. He did not smile at lunch. "No parade," he said again and again.

Wei Chou wished that Uncle Li would smile. That afternoon she had an idea.

She rode her bike to Amy's house. "Meet me at the picnic table in the park," Wei Chou said. "Bring everyone you can find. Tell them to bring their New Year's costumes. Tell Timmie to bring his drum, too."

Wei Chou went back to her house. She found some crayons, some colored paper, and some scissors. She put them all into a big paper bag with her costume. Then she ran out the front door.

Her friends were waiting in the park. "Let's have a parade," she said to them. "Let's put on our costumes. We can be a dragon. I will make the mask."

She drew a dragon's head on the paper bag with her crayons. Then she cut two small holes for the eyes. She made a large hole for the mouth. Wei Chou's friends made little flags from the colored paper.

"We are ready," said Wei Chou.

The children made a line. Wei Chou put on the mask. Amy was the last in line. She was the dragon's tail.

Timmie began to play his drum. The children waved their flags. The dragon moved forward down the sidewalk. People came out of their houses to see it.

Officer Butler saw the dragon. "Where is this snake going?" he asked.

"This is not a snake," said Wei Chou. "This is a dragon. We are having a New Year's parade."

"Then I will lead the parade," Officer Butler said.

Uncle Li and Wei Chou's parents were standing in the yard. The puppy was sitting in the grass. They saw the dragon and the children in their costumes.

Uncle Li was smiling. He ran to meet them. "Now all we need are some fireworks," he said.

Wei Chou's puppy ran after the dragon. He barked loudly.

Uncle Li turned around. "We do not need anything now," he said. "That puppy sounds enough like fireworks!"

Wei Chou laughed and said, "Shin Nee-an Kie Lo," which means "Happy New Year."

"You have made me very happy," said Uncle Li. "Each Chinese year has a name. This is the Year of the Dragon, but I will call it the Year of the Smile."

1. What did Wei Chou do to make the celebration special?

2. What did Wei Chou and her mother do to get the house ready?

3. Where did you learn that Uncle Li was unhappy all morning?

4. How did Wei Chou make Uncle Li happy?

Think about how Wei Chou made Uncle Li smile. What could you do to make a sad person smile again? Write four sentences that tell things you might do to make someone smile.

227

How do people in different countries make the first day of a new year a day to remember?

New Year's Day

by Martha and Charles Shapp

People all over the world celebrate the beginning of a new year. Most people celebrate the first of January as New Year's Day.

Other people celebrate New Year's Day at different times of the year. In some countries New Year's Day is celebrated in the spring when the flowers begin to bloom. All people do not celebrate New Year's Day at the same time, but they all celebrate the beginning of the new year in some way.

The celebration often starts on New Year's Eve. This is the last night of the old year.

On New Year's Eve, many people celebrate by having parties at home. At midnight the old year ends, and the new year begins. People shake hands or kiss, and everybody shouts, "Happy New Year!"

Some people meet in the streets to bring in the new year. They laugh and sing and blow horns. In some cities, people in the street join hands and sing "Auld Lang Syne" at midnight.

In parts of Africa, people greet the new year with dances. The children of Scotland have lots of fun on New Year's Eve. They go from house to house and sing songs. The people of Mexico celebrate the new year with a big fiesta, or party.

In some countries, people open their doors wide just before midnight on New Year's Eve. They do this to let the old year out and the new year in.

Some people believe that they must make a "clean start" for the new year. They give their homes a good cleaning before the new year comes. Other people make a clean start by pouring clean water on their heads.

Some people get ready for the new year by throwing away their old dishes. They get new dishes for the new year.

Chinese people all over the world celebrate New Year's Day with parades. The Chinese New Year's Day comes in February. A big, make-believe dragon has an important part in this parade.

Parades are also held in cities all across the United States. In one city, people dress up in funny costumes. Then they parade through the streets.

Roses grow in California in January. So, a city in California celebrates with a Parade of Roses.

Different people celebrate New Year's Day at different times and in different ways. However, all around the world, people celebrate the beginning of a new year.

1. How do people make New Year's Day a day to remember?

2. What are two times of the year that New Year's Day is celebrated?

3. What do all people do on New Year's Day?

4. Where did you read what children in Scotland do on New Year's Eve?

People celebrate many days during the year. Think about a day you like to celebrate. Write a paragraph that tells what that day is and how you celebrate it.

The New Year

by Jane W. Krows

A brand New Year arrived last night;
It came while I was waiting.
But I did not hear the horns or shouts
Of people celebrating.
Because, you see, I fell asleep
Before the hour, when
The old year silently passed out
And the New Year entered in.
But I have a clean new calendar
Which hangs before my eyes
And every day that's listed
Will hold a new surprise.

Compound Words

How many words do you see in the word *bluebird*? Yes, there are two words in *bluebird*. The word *bluebird* is a **compound word**. It is made up of the two words *blue* and *bird*. If you can read both of the words, then you can read the compound word.

What is blue? Blue is a color. What is a bird? A bird is an animal that can fly. Now you know that a bluebird is a blue animal that can fly.

Read the following sentence. Look for the compound word.

Mary went to the bookstore.

The compound word is *bookstore*. What are the two words in *bookstore*? The two words are *book* and *store*. What do you think Mary would buy at the bookstore? Mary would buy books at a bookstore.

Now read the following sentences. Look for the compound word in each sentence. What two words make up each compound word? What does each compound word mean?

1. John took his raincoat with him.
2. We went for a ride in the rowboat.
3. Clyde's bedroom was a cave.
4. The chair is in front of the toybox.

When you see a compound word, look for the two words that make up the compound word. If you know both of these words, then you will know the meaning of the compound word. See how many compound words you can find in the next selection.

This is a very old story about a small town in the state of Delaware. People who live in the town now are still telling this story. What happened to the town?

Cornstalks and Cannonballs

by Barbara Mitchell

Long ago there was a little town by the sea. It was called Lewes (LOO-iss). Lewes was a pretty town. Fishing boats filled the bay. Sea birds flew. Sea winds blew.

238

Lewes was a nice town. Fishermen got up before the sun to go fishing. Farmers worked hard in their fields. All the people were very happy in their little town.

One winter day, the fishermen came home with some bad news. English ships were in the bay. There were many cannons on these ships. England and the United States were fighting again!

The English would not let any other ships into Delaware Bay. They also would not let any boats out. The fishermen could not work. All day they sat and talked and worried and wondered. Everyone watched and waited. They waited for a very long time.

The sailors on the ships didn't have much food left. They told one of their captains, "Sir John, we want meat! We want vegetables! We want to eat!"

So Sir John sat down and wrote a note.

To the people of Lewes, Delaware:

Send us meat, Send us vegetables. If you don't, we will fire on your town.

Sir John thought that the little town would be afraid. "Soon we will be eating meat and vegetables," he told his sailors.

The people of Lewes were not afraid. They were angry. "Send you our meat and vegetables?" they said. "Never! We will never feed you!"

When Sir John did not get the food, he could not believe it! He wondered what to do next.

The people of Lewes did not sit still. "We will fight!" they said. "Sam Davis will be our captain."

"Let's clean up the old cannons!" someone said. They cleaned up four old cannons. Then the little town waited in the dark. The English didn't fire on the town.

A few weeks later, Sir John's sailors were just about out of food. "Where is our meat? Where are our vegetables?" they shouted. So Sir John sent another note to the town.

I will give you one last chance. Send us food right now, or else!

The people of the town still did not send food to the sailors. Sir John was even more angry now. "Ready! Fire!" he shouted.

Cannonballs flew at the little town. The English fired fast. The people of Lewes did not fire as fast. They did not have many cannonballs.

Then the people of Lewes fired their last cannonball. The farmers looked at the fishermen. The fishermen looked at the farmers. They all looked at the beach. It was covered with cannonballs that the English had just fired. Sam Davis said, "Let me see one of those cannonballs."

He took the ball to a cannon. The
ball went right in. The English
cannonballs fit the town cannons!

"Call out the boys!" Sam Davis
shouted. They all came running. He
told them to get the cannonballs on the
beach and carry them to the cannons.
Then the people of Lewes fired the
cannonballs back at the English ships.

Sam Davis was still worried. He knew
his little town was not as strong as the
English ships. He looked at the farmers'
fields. He saw dry cornstalks coming up
through the snow. Suddenly he smiled.

Then he shouted to the farmers, "Bring me those cornstalks! Bring me your farm tools! We are going to make a fire!"

"Farm tools?" asked the farmers. They did as they were told.

While the farmers were gone, Sam Davis made a fire. When the farmers came back, he took a hoe. He held the hoe close to the fire. He held it just close enough to make it black.

"Make all the tools and cornstalks black," Sam told the men.

That night, Sir John said, "The town is out of cannonballs. Get out the rowboats. We will row to the beach and take over."

"Look, Sir!" shouted a sailor. People were filling the town. They came down the streets and across the beaches.

They were the people of the little town. Some of them were women dressed as men. In the dark, Sir John could not tell the men from the women. It looked as if they all carried guns. Those guns were really just cornstalks and hoes and sticks and brooms that had been made black.

"Look at all the people! They have guns!" shouted a sailor.

"There are too many people for us to fight! Go back to the ships!" Sir John yelled.

So the English sailors went back to their ships. They sailed away. They never came back.

The fishermen went back to their fishing. The farmers picked up their tools and went back to their farms.

The sea birds flew and the sea winds blew in that brave little town of long ago.

1. What happened to Lewes, Delaware?

2. What made the people of Lewes very angry?

3. What clues tell why "Cornstalks and Cannonballs" is a good title for this story?

4. What did you think of Sam Davis' plan to fool the English?

Cornstalks and *cannonballs* are both compound words from the story. Use some of these compound words to write a short story: *cornstalks, sunshine, fisherman, sunflower, sailboat,* and *rowboat.*

*This is the story of an old quilt.
What are some of the things that
happened to the quilt?*

The Quilt Story

by Tony Johnston

Long ago, a little girl's mother made
a quilt to keep the girl warm when the
snow came down. The mother sewed the
quilt by a yellow flame. As she sewed,
she hummed. She stitched the tails of
falling stars on the quilt. She also stitched
the name Abigail on it.

Abigail loved the quilt. She wrapped it around her in the quiet dark and watched the winter skies.

Sometimes Abigail played in the woods near her home. She had milk. Her dolls had milk. The quilt had milk all over it.

Sometimes Abigail pretended the quilt was a gown. She put it on when she pretended to ride her horse to town. The quilt ripped. So her mother fixed it.

When Abigail played hide-and-seek with her sisters, she hid under the quilt. She was quiet, but her sisters still found her.

Abigail slept under the quilt when she was sick. It kept her warm.

One day Abigail's family moved away,
across wide rivers and over a rock-hard
trail. The quilt went too. It was not
stuffed into the trunks. It kept Abigail and
her sisters warm from the wild winds. It
kept them warm from the rain and the
cold nights.

Abigail's father built a new house in
the woods. He built Abigail a new bed.
He made her a new wooden horse, too.
When Abigail's father was finished,
everyone said, "Welcome home."

Abigail felt sad. They had a new house, a new horse, and a new bed. Everything was new, except the quilt. So Abigail's mother rocked her as mothers do. Then she tucked her in, and Abigail felt at home again under the quilt.

One day when the quilt was very old and very loved, Abigail folded it carefully and put it in the attic. Many years passed. Everyone forgot the quilt was in the attic.

A raccoon came and loved the quilt.
It dug a hole in it with its black paws.
The raccoon hid some food there.

A cat came and loved the quilt. It rolled
on the stars, and the stuffing spilled out
like snow. Then the cat rolled up in the
snow and purred.

"Kitty, Kitty," called a little girl. She
found her cat, and she found the quilt.
The little girl wrapped the quilt around her.
She loved it, too.

"Can you make it like new?" she asked
her mother. So her mother fixed the holes.
She pushed fresh stuffing into the quilt. She
stitched long tails on the stars to swish
across the quilt again.

One day the little girl's family moved
miles and miles away.

Her family found a new house. It was freshly cleaned and freshly painted. The family unpacked and unpacked all night. When they were finished, everyone said, "Welcome home."

The little girl felt sad. Everything was new, except the quilt. So the little girl's mother rocked her as mothers do. Then she tucked her in, and the little girl felt at home again under the quilt.

1. What things happened to the quilt?

2. How did the little girls and the animals feel about the quilt? Why?

3. How did you feel when the raccoon made a hole in the quilt? Why?

4. Where in the story did you know how the second little girl felt about the quilt?

Pretend you are going to move to a new place. Write a story about something you might take with you to help you feel at home. Tell why you picked what you did.

Arthur is selling all of his old toys. There is one toy that is very special to him. Who buys that toy? How does Arthur feel after it is sold?

Arthur's Honey Bear

story and pictures by Lillian Hoban

It was spring-cleaning day. Violet was cleaning out her toy chest. She made two piles of toys — one to keep, and one to put away. Arthur was sticking stamps into his stamp book.

"I am going to clean out my toy chest, too," said Arthur. "Then I am going to have a Tag Sale."

258

"What is a Tag Sale?" asked Violet.

"A Tag Sale is a sale you have to sell your old junk," said Arthur.

"I don't have any old junk," said Violet. "I want to keep all of my toys."

"When I was little," said Arthur, "I wanted to keep all of my toys, too. Now I want to sell some of them." Arthur began to clean out his toy chest. He took a pile of toys to the back steps.

Arthur took his Hula-Hoop, his Yo-Yo, and a pile of finger paintings. He took Noah's Ark, his baby King Kong, his sandbox set, his Old Maid cards, and his rocks and marbles. Then he took out his Honey Bear.

"Father gave me Honey Bear when I had the chicken pox," said Arthur. "Honey Bear always tasted my medicine for me when I was sick." Arthur moved Honey Bear behind baby King Kong.

"Now I will make the price tags," said Arthur.

"Let me help," said Violet.

"You can cut the paper for the tags," said Arthur, "and I will write the prices."

Arthur made a big sign. It said:

Then Arthur marked the prices on the tags. He put tags on all the toys and pictures and rocks and marbles.

"You didn't put a tag on Honey Bear," said Violet.

"He is in very good shape," said Arthur. "He has only one eye missing. Maybe I should sell him for a lot of money. Maybe I should sell him for thirty-one cents."

"His ear is falling off," said Violet.

"Well," said Arthur, "I have not made up my mind yet." He moved Honey Bear all the way behind baby King Kong.

"Now," said Arthur, "we have to make arrows. Then everyone will know where the sale is."

Violet cut arrow shapes out of paper. Arthur wrote "Tag Sale" on them.

Arthur and Violet hung the arrows on trees. "Now we will wait for someone to come and buy," said Arthur. They waited and waited.

"Here comes Wilma. Maybe she will buy something," said Violet.

"Friday is my sister's birthday," said
Wilma. "Do you have anything good?"

"Well," said Arthur, "here is a very nice
Hula-Hoop."

"It's bent," said Wilma, "and my sister
has a Hula-Hoop. How much is the bear?"

"What bear?" asked Arthur.

"The bear behind baby King Kong," said
Wilma. "He doesn't have a price tag."

"Oh," said Arthur quickly, "he costs a lot."

"Well, how much?" asked Wilma.

"Your sister won't like him," said Arthur. "She is too old for stuffed toys."

"No, she isn't," said Wilma. "She takes her stuffed pig to bed with her."

"Well," said Arthur, "I will sell him to you for fifty cents."

"All right," said Wilma. She took fifty cents out of her pocket.

"Do you gift wrap?" asked Wilma.

"No," said Arthur.

"Well," said Wilma, "I don't have money for wrapping paper. If I buy a present at the toy store, they will gift wrap for nothing." Wilma put the fifty cents back in her pocket and walked away.

Arthur looked at Honey Bear and hugged
him. He held Honey Bear.

"I wish someone would buy *something*,"
said Arthur.

Violet said, "I will buy something,
Arthur. I will buy your Honey Bear."

"You don't have any money," said Arthur.

"I have thirty-one cents," said Violet. "I
can give you thirty-one cents and my
brand-new Color-Me-Nice coloring book.
None of the pictures are colored in yet."

"Well, maybe," said Arthur, "but maybe I want to keep Honey Bear for myself."

"I thought you said you don't want to keep your old junk," said Violet.

"Honey Bear is not old junk," said Arthur. "He is my special bear."

"I will give you thirty-one cents, my Color-Me-Nice coloring book, and my box of crayons," said Violet. "Only the purple one is broken."

"Honey Bear has been my bear for a long time," said Arthur. "He wants me to take care of him."

"I will give you thirty-one cents, my coloring book, my crayons, and the prize from the box of cereal we ate this morning," said Violet.

"Well, all right," said Arthur. So Violet
gave Arthur thirty-one cents, her crayons,
her coloring book, and the prize from the
box of cereal. Arthur gave Violet his Honey
Bear.

Arthur took all of his sale things and put
them away. He put the thirty-one cents in
his mailbox bank. Then he colored a picture
in his Color-Me-Nice coloring book. He
colored a picture of a boy holding a bear.

Violet came in holding Honey Bear. He
was dressed in a pink tutu. He was wearing
a necklace and a hat.

"Honey Bear is a *boy*!" said Arthur. "He does not like those clothes."

"Honey Bear is my bear now," said Violet. "I will dress him the way I want."

"You don't know how to take care of him," said Arthur.

"Well, I am his mother now," said Violet, "and I am taking care of him."

"I think Honey Bear misses me," said Arthur. "He wishes he were still *my* bear."

"Well, he's not," said Violet. She took Honey Bear for a walk.

Arthur sat down and opened the
Color-Me-Nice coloring book again. Then
he hummed a little tune, and thought for a
while. Violet came back. She sat down with
Honey Bear. Arthur thought some more.
Then he said to Violet, "Violet, are you my
little sister?"

"Yes," said Violet.

"Well then, do you know what I am?"
asked Arthur.

"You are my big brother," said Violet.

"Yes, I am," said Arthur, "and do you
know what that means?"

"No," said Violet.

"That means I am Honey Bear's *uncle!*" said Arthur. Arthur picked up Honey Bear and hugged him. "I am your uncle, Honey Bear," said Arthur. "I will always be your uncle. Do you know what uncles do?" said Arthur to Honey Bear.

"What do uncles do?" asked Violet.

"Uncles play with their nephews, and take them out for treats," said Arthur.

"Honey Bear likes treats," said Violet. "Can I come, too?"

"All right," said Arthur.

Arthur took the thirty-one cents out of his mailbox bank. Then he and Violet and Honey Bear went out for a treat.

Honey Bear sat on his Uncle Arthur's lap. "Honey Bear, I am glad I will always be your uncle," said Arthur.

1. Who bought Arthur's Honey Bear?

2. How did Arthur feel after he sold Honey Bear? Why?

3. Why did Arthur have a Tag Sale?

4. How did Arthur get over missing Honey Bear?

5. When did you first think that Arthur did not want to sell Honey Bear?

Thinking About "Scrapbooks"

In "Scrapbooks," you read about special celebrations and things that are fun to remember. You found out some things that people like to put into scrapbooks. You learned about how people all over the world celebrate the beginning of a new year. You read about how the people of Lewes, Delaware, saved their town. You followed the story of a quilt that was passed from one family to another.

As you read other stories, look for the special times people want to remember. What do the people do to remember these times?

1. How did the boy in "Grandma Without Me" and Wei Chou make someone in their families happy?

2. What special day might the people of Lewes, Delaware, celebrate?

3. How is Abigail's quilt like a scrapbook?

4. What do you think Arthur would save in a scrapbook to help him remember Honey Bear?

Read on Your Own

Gung Hay Fat Choy by June Behrens. Childrens Press. This book tells all about the Chinese New Year. There are many colorful pictures.

Arthur's Pen Pal by Lillian Hoban. Harper. At first, Arthur wishes that he could trade sisters. Later, he decides he'd like to keep things the way they are.

Arthur's Prize Reader by Lillian Hoban. Harper. Arthur loses the Super Chimp reading contest. When Arthur helps his sister win the contest, they both get a prize.

Odd Jobs and Friends by Tony Johnston. Putnam. Odd Jobs is a boy who will try to do any job.

The Quilt by Ann Jonas. Greenwillow. A girl gets a new patchwork quilt that helps her remember many wonderful things.

My Island Grandma by Kathryn Lasky. Warne. A girl tells about all the things she does when she spends some time with her grandmother.

The Star-Spangled Banner by Peter Spier. Doubleday. This book tells the story of how Francis Scott Key wrote the song during the War of 1812.

Chin Chiang and the Dragon's Dance by Ian Wallace. Atheneum. A young boy is afraid to do the dragon's dance for the Chinese New Year celebration.

Glossary

The glossary is a special dictionary for this book. To find a word, use alphabetical, or ABC, order. For example, to find the word *swing* in the glossary, first look for the part of the glossary that has words beginning with the letter *s*. Then find the entry word, *swing*. The glossary gives the meaning of the word as it is used in the book. Then the word is used in a sentence.

Sometimes different forms of the word follow the sentence. If a different form of the word, such as *swung*, is used in the book, then that word is used in the sentence.

A small blue box ■ at the end of the entry means that there is a picture to go with that word.

A

attic   the part of a house just under the roof: The large boxes were in the *attic*.

B

badge   a pin that is a sign that someone does a kind of work: Her *badge* shows what her job is.

band   people who play together for a parade: The sound of the *band* playing told people the parade was starting.

bank   a place to keep money: He put ten cents in his *bank*. ■

bark   **1.** the sound made by a dog: I heard a *bark*. **2.** to make a dog sound: The dog *barked* at the cat. **barks, barked**

barn   a farm building: The cows are in the *barn*. ■

baseball   a ball game with nine players: She pastes pictures of the *baseball* game in her book.

beach   land on the edge of water: We can bring the boat up on the *beach*.

bifocals   glasses with which people can see things that are near and things that are far away: His *bifocals* let him look up from his book and watch for the mail carrier. **bifocals**

277

blank   free of writing: She wanted to write in the *blank* notebook.

blind   cannot see: *Blind* people sometimes have Seeing Eye dogs.

brave   not afraid: She was *brave* to fly the plane through the rain.

brook   a waterway smaller than a river: He could catch many fish in the *brook*.

broom   a brush at the end of a long pole: They used *brooms* to sweep the house. **brooms** ■

build   to put things together: The people *built* the barn. **built**

bus   something in which many people ride from place to place: We will ride to the next town on the *bus*.

C

card   heavy paper with something printed on it: They put the words to remember on *cards*. **cards**

cent   a penny: She gave him ten *cents* for the book. **cents**

clock   something used to tell time: We see by the *clock* that it is time to eat. ■

cocoon   a covering for a caterpillar: This *cocoon* shows us that one day there will be a butterfly.

cold not hot: The snow and ice came when it was *cold.*

collect to bring things together: He wanted a notebook to use to *collect* stories. **collects**

costume special clothes: She was wearing a clown *costume.* **costumes**

cow a farm animal that gives milk: Many *cows* live on a farm. **cows**

cup a small bowl from which people drink: He put the water in a *cup.*

D

deer an animal that lives in the forest: The *deer* came out of the forest to get water. ■

detective a person who tries to get information to help people solve problems: The *detective* wanted to find out who took the paintings.

E

egg something that holds a baby bird until it is ready to hatch: The chicken sat on two *eggs.* **eggs** ■

electricity something that makes lights work: The lights went off when we lost our *electricity.*

eve the night before: They had a party on New Year's *Eve.*

F

family a person's mother, father, brothers, and sisters: She came back to town to see her *family.*

fee money given to pay for something: He was given a *fee* for his work.

fence something put up to close in some land: They put up a *fence* to keep the dog in the yard. ■

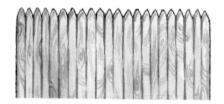

fiesta a party: The most important part of the celebration was the *fiesta.*

fireplace an open place in a room where a fire may be made: We built a fire in the *fireplace* to keep warm.

flame a bright part of a fire: The *flame* could be seen from the road.

frame 1. the outside edge of eye glasses: She wanted glasses with blue *frames.*
2. the outside edge of a picture: The *frame* makes the picture look bigger. **frames**

front before someone or something: Their van was at the *front* of the parade.

G

gas not a solid or a liquid: The rain turned into a *gas* when the weather got warm.

geese more than one goose: The *geese* were bigger than the chickens.

gerbil a small animal that looks something like a mouse: He took his *gerbil* to school to show everyone. ■

glasses eyeglasses; something that people wear to help them see better: I can see small letters when I wear my new *glasses.*

gown a special dress: The woman wanted a new *gown* for the party.

grandmother your mother's or father's mother: We went to see our *grandmother* on Sunday.

greet to meet and speak to in a friendly way: The brothers came to *greet* their father. **greets, greeted**

groundhog a small animal that has brown or gray fur and small legs: People come to the zoo to see the *groundhog* on his special day. ■

gym a place to play games and work out: We played ball in the *gym* today.

H

---

hall a place used to get from room to room: His room was at the end of the *hall.*

hatch to come out of an egg: A baby chicken will *hatch* from each egg. **hatches, hatched**

heat to make something hot: We should *heat* the food before we eat it.

hide-and-seek a game played by children: The best game they played at the party was *hide-and-seek.*

hoe something used to do farm work: The farmer put his *hoe* in the barn. ■

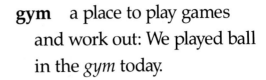

hose   a long tube used to bring water to plants and flowers: I will pull the *hose* to the flowers at the back of the house.

huge   very large: He rode into the field on a *huge* tractor.

L
---

lake   water with land around it: We saw the lights of the boats out on the *lake*.

law   a rule that people follow: Everyone should learn the *laws* of the town. **laws**

library   a place where books are kept: He went to the *library* to get a book on forecasting.

line   a long mark made on paper: She wanted to draw a *line* on both ends of her paper. **lines**

luck   something good that happens without a plan: He thought the ladybug would give him *luck*.

M
---

machine   something that people use to do work: A truck is a *machine* that may be used on a farm.

marbles   small glass balls that people play with: The boys have many different kinds of *marbles*.

marsh   wet land: Ducks often live in a *marsh*.

mask   a covering for the face: She put on a lion *mask* for the party. ■

meat   the part of an animal that people eat: We got *meat* and cheese to eat from the farmer.

medicine   something taken by people or animals to make them well: She took the *medicine* three times a day when she was sick.

midnight   twelve hours after noon: The new day starts at *midnight*.

mile   5,280 feet: It is two *miles* from town to the farm. **miles**

money   change or paper that is made to be used to pay for things: He took *money* to pay for the milk. ■

moon   something people see as a light in the night sky: The forecaster says we will see a full *moon* tonight.

N

news   important things that happen: He wanted to hear the *news* each morning.

O

outdoor   outside in the open: They went to the *outdoor* art show.

P

patch   a small piece: There was a *patch* of ice near the pond.

pen   **1.** a place with a fence around it: We keep the pig in a *pen*.   **2.** something people use to write: I need a *pen* to write in my notebook.

pets   animals that live with people: Dogs and cats are good *pets*.

pin a small hard wire with a point: She used a *pin* to hold the flower on her dress. ■

pipes tubes that carry water: There was ice on the *pipes* outside the house.

planet a body that moves around the sun: Earth is the *planet* on which we live.

pretend to make believe: He liked to *pretend* he was a prince. **pretended**

prince the son of a king and queen: People told about the *prince* in a legend.

prize something people win: He was given the toy as a *prize*.

pupa one part of the life of a butterfly: The caterpillar is called a *pupa* when it is inside its cocoon.

Q

quilt a covering for a bed made from many different bits of cloth: They worked a year to make the *quilt*. ■

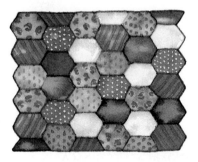

R

ready to be all set to do something: The airplane was *ready* to land.

rescue something done to save people or things: Ben came to the *rescue* of the cat.

ring **1.** the sound made by a bell: They could hear the *ring* of the bell. **2.** to make a bell sound: She wanted to *ring* the bell. **rings, ringing**

rose   **1.** a flower: He gave the girl a *rose*.   **2.** got up: He *rose* from his bed.

row   **1.** one after another: The people sat all in a *row*.   **2.** to make a boat move: The boy started to *row* the boat.

S
---

sack   a bag: She took the prize to the party in a *sack*. ■

sail   to use the wind to move a boat: They wanted to *sail* out to sea in a boat. **sailed**

sailor   a person who works on a ship: The *sailor* worked on a large ship.

send   to make something go from one place to another: She wanted to *send* a letter to her father. **sends, sending, sent**

shadow   a dark spot that is seen when light is blocked: When the sun comes up, my *shadow* gets longer.

sharp   very clear: She could see a *sharp* picture.

sick   ill, not well: He ate too much and got *sick*.

silk   a fine cloth: The blue pajamas were made of *silk*.

sing   to make pretty sounds: People come to listen when we *sing*. **sang, sung**

skin   a covering on the outside of something: The sun feels warm on my *skin*.

song   sounds made by singing: The *songs* of the people were part of the celebration. **songs**

spin   to turn around: The toy top *spins* very fast. **spins, spun**

spring   the time of the year that follows winter: Rain helps flowers grow in the *spring*.

stamp   a small, printed piece of paper: He needed a *stamp* to mail his letter. ■

state   a part of the United States: He can mail his letter to any *state* in the United States.

stove   a place to burn wood or coal to heat a room: Put some more wood in the *stove*. ■

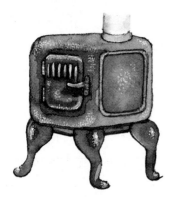

stuffing   something used for filling: Everybody wanted more of the turkey *stuffing*.

swan   a large, beautiful water bird: The people watched when the *swan* flew to the pond.

T
---

team   a group of people who work or play together: They played ball on the same *team*.

teeth   parts of the body inside the mouth used to bite food: The dog uses his *teeth* to get his bone.

tool   an instrument to do work: She used her *tools* to build a fence. **tools**

trail   a path: The cart tipped over on the *trail*.

trash   things people throw away: He put the old newspapers in the *trash*.

trip   1. to fall over something: The rock in the path made me *trip*.   2. a move from one place to another: He went on a plane *trip*.

trunk   1. the bottom part of a tree: The animal ran up the *trunk* of the tree. ■

2. a box used to store things: She put her old clothes in a *trunk*.

tune   sounds of a song: He heard the pretty *tune* from far away.

tutu   a short dress used in dancing: Her costume for the show was a blue *tutu*. ■

U

upset   not feeling well: He was *upset* when he heard the bad news.

V

vegetable   a plant used as food: The foods she liked best were *vegetables*.
vegetables

visit   1. to come to see: He *visits* his mother every day.
visits   2. a time when a person comes to see someone else: They came for a short *visit*.

W

weather   what it is like outside: We will go out on the boat when the *weather* is good.

week   seven days: My birthday is in a *week*.

wheat   a cereal plant: We eat *wheat* cereal every morning.

wing   a part of an animal or thing that is used to fly: The bird has large *wings*.

wings ■

winter   the part of the year that follows fall: There is ice on the pond in *winter*.

wooden   made of wood: The house has a *wooden* fence around it.

woods   a forest: The small animals lived deep in the *woods*.

wrong   not right: He turned down the *wrong* road.

_____
Y
_____

yard   ground next to a school or home: We played ball in his *yard*.

young   not old: The *young* boy played ball with his mother.

yo-yo   a toy that runs up and down on a string: He broke the string on his *yo-yo*. ■

Word List

The following words are introduced in this book. Each is listed beside the number of the page on which it first appears.

Watch Out, Ronald Morgan!
(4–11)

4 Ronald Morgan
  superkid
  yard
  Rosemary
  hung
  Frank
  gerbil
5 Goldie
  Billy
  winter
  Miss Tyler
6 Tom
  Marc
  Doctor Sims
  Michael
  point
7 sharp
  clear
  ready
8 threw
  Jimmy
9 Alice
  wearing
  throw
10 hey
  super

Benjamin Franklin's Glasses
(12–17)

12 Benjamin
  Franklin
  discovered
  printer
  electricity
  write
  even
  laws
  United States
14 hotter
15 older
  pair
16 bifocals
  kept

Nick Joins In
(18–27)

18 Nick
  joins
  teacher
  parents
  wheelchair
  else
19 spilled
  Wednesday
20 spoke
  Mrs. Becker
  Rachel
  because
  Timmie
22 gym
  windows
24 edge
  roof
  Ben
26 rescue
  excuse

Draw Conclusions
(30–31)

30 draw
  conclusions
  given
  clues
  paragraph
  gifts
  party
31 Peter
  different
  understand
  selection

Illustrators

Mike Adams: 80-83; Lynn Uhde Adams: 192-193; Robert Baumgartner: 116-124; Dave Blanchette: 30-31, 208-209; Alex Block: 4-10; Kay Chorao: 68-74; Eulala Connor: 132-140, 202; Virginia Curtain: 234-235; Jim Deigan: 104-108; Tommie dePaola: 250-256; Lane Dupont: 156-164; Andrea Eberbach: 176-182; Ethel Gold: 44-45, 98-99; Lillian Hoban: 258-270; Syd Hoff: 46-52; Joe Lasker: 18-26; Arnold Lobel: 110-114; Mike Muir: 218-226; Jim Noble: 154-155; Michael O'Reilly: 277-288; Tom Powers: 84; Gail Roth: 28-29; S.D. Schindler: 210-211; Bob Shein: 174-175; Dan Siculan: 12-16, 238-248; Blanche Sims: 32-42; Joel Snyder: 76-78, 167, 236-237; Joe Veno: 86-96; Judith Vigna: 200-206; Justin Wager: 142-152, 228-232; Lane Yerkes: 54-55.

HBJ maps and charts: pp. 101, 103.

7
8
D 9
E 0
F 1
G 2
H 3
I 4
J 5